ALL ABOUT INVESTING IN REAL ESTATE SECURITIES

ALL ABOUT INVESTING IN REAL ESTATE SECURITIES

by IRA U. COBLEIGH

WEYBRIGHT AND TALLEY

New York

ALL ABOUT INVESTING IN REAL ESTATE
SECURITIES

Published in the United States by
WEYBRIGHT AND TALLEY
750 Third Avenue   New York, New York 10017

LIBRARY OF CONGRESS CATALOG CARD NUMBER: 75-165093

MANUFACTURED IN THE UNITED STATES OF AMERICA

Preface

REAL estate has been man's favorite investment since his eviction from the Garden of Eden. Over thousands of years it has created more personal fortunes for more people than any other form of property. For 58 million Americans, the purchase of a home is the most important single investment they ever make. Individuals seeking income producing and gainful investments as their incomes and surplus funds increase, also consider the purchase of real estate, along with stocks and other marketable securities, after they have built their financial foundations with prudent amounts in savings accounts and life insurance. Many people augment their home ownership by the purchase of a vacation cottage, or a few southern or southwestern acres as speculations or possible retirement homesites.

However, much as he might like to own more real estate, particularly in an inflationary era, the average solvent American finds realty investing complicated and burdensome. If he acquires a two-family house or a multiple dwelling, there are always the problems of management, maintenance, repair, landscaping, or taxes. Individual dealing in real estate indeed requires personal attention to a series of nagging details: taxes, assessment, zoning, title search and clearance, insurance, boundaries, easements, and the intricate legal niceties of conveying, leasing or mortgaging property. All of these things which are connected with property management and dealing with (and trying to please) tenants—the usual requirements for large amounts of capital, plus frequently, the inability to find a satisfactory buyer when you want or need to sell—have effectively prevented widespread and diversified ownership of real estate among individuals.

Enthusiasm for investment in favorably located real property, however, persists. This book is designed to implement, and possibly to reward, that enthusiasm by outlining the many attractive ways in which you can participate in ownership of real estate or high-yielding mortgages through the medium of marketable securities: shares of stock or trust certificates. These securities involve no details of management or supervision and require very little attention on your part; they can be easily bought, sold, quoted, or used as collateral for loans. In addition, they may provide you with dependable and even generous income, unique tax shelter, and high leverage; together with attractive opportunities for sizeable capital gains derived from equity interests in substantial modern office buildings, motels, high-rise apartments, shopping centers, etc. —properties in which ownership interests were formerly available only to wealthy individuals, syndicates, and large corporations.

The long-range economies of real estate are indeed most attractive. The prices of well-located land and sound income-producing structures have been in an almost uninterrupted rising trend throughout the civilized world for the past 300 years. "We're still making people, but we've stopped making land." Good luck, and may you become land rich after the manner of Texas ranchers, the Astors, Vanderbilts, the Goelets, and the late Arthur Vining Davis, who honeycombed Florida with his land holdings.

Contents

It is a comfortable feeling to know that you stand on your own ground. Land is about the only thing that can't fly away.

—ANTHONY TROLLOPE

ALL ABOUT INVESTING
IN REAL ESTATE
SECURITIES

CHAPTER I

The Eternal Desirability of Real Estate

IN his provocative book, *The Territorial Imperative,* Robert Ardrey showed that among animals and birds there exists a powerful instinct to stake out, claim, and occupy areas for individual or group possession and to use areas with boundaries invisibly defined but apparently understood both by members of the group and by outsiders; all resolutely defended against invaders and interlopers. Man apparently shares with lower animals this possessive territorial instinct. His earliest conception of private property began with the patch of land he and his family occupied, whether it was cave, jungle, desert, plain or waterside.

The great early civilizations of the Egyptians, Babylonians, Chinese, and Persians centered around the possession of the rich agricultural lands which formed in the valleys of great rivers. Nations flourished and floundered as they acquired and improved, or lost control of, broad and strategic land areas across the world. Land has always been the essential foundation for the wealth. of nations, cities, states, tribes, family groups, and individuals. Since primitive times the ownership of most land areas has increasingly gravitated to tribal and religious groups, and to political subdivisions and nations. Subjects, citizens, slaves, or tenants worked the soil, tended the herds or dug in the mines and quarries.

Just because people and nations occupied land areas and established boundaries did not mean that they could keep

1

them indefinitely. Far from it! Over the past 4000 years land
ownership has been constantly contested. Especially in Europe and the Near East, territory has changed hands repeat-
edly, as predatory foreign hordes invaded and subjugated the
lands of the less powerful, more peaceful or declining peoples,
and claimed title to this conquered terrain as a matter of
course.

The Babylonians lost out to the Assyrians, the Assyrians
were conquered by the Persians. Alexander the Great conquered for Macedonia all of the land area from Greece to the
gates of India, including Egypt; then he generously parceled
out great sections of this broad terrain to several of his gen-
erals before he died. After Alexander came the Romans; then
the German tribes tore the Roman Empire apart; and ownership of parts of the Rhine and Danube Valleys has been a
migrant-military door prize during almost every century since
Caesar Augustus.

On this side of the Atlantic, retention of land by the original claimants and owners was equally impossible. The
French, English, and Dutch colonists took over North America, while the Spaniards through the use of force became the
new owners of most of Mexico and large parts of Central and
South America.

The Incas proved to have no greater ability in defending
their home and living space than the Iroquois or the Apaches.
Tens of millions of acres of the New World changed ownership by virtue of military prowess.

During all this myriad transfer of title either by force or
fraud throughout the centuries, land everywhere, except in
mountains, deserts, forests, and jungles, tended to become
more valuable as populations expanded, and definitions and
assertion of ownership and boundaries became increasingly
important. As surging populations urgently required ever
more land, improvements, and structures, the building of
houses and great edifices became a major economic activity;

from ancient tombs and public buildings to amphitheaters, and roads and bridges to connect the population centers; then came the majestic cathedrals, palaces, auditoriums, seaports followed in due course by railways, skyscrapers, high-rise apartments, Radio Cities and Pittsburgh Triangles.

Along the way as peoples endeavored to free themselves from the yoke of autocratic monarchs, feudalism, and the political and financial dominance of the Church of Rome, there developed broadened ownership of realty by individuals. (In Spain and certain South American countries today, the largest property owner outside the government is still the Roman Catholic Church). Clamor for "land reform" grew as people became better educated and demanded their rights through increased application of democratic processes in political action.

The foregoing capsuled summary of significant historical trends in territorial possession seems appropriate as: 1. a prelude to the economic evalution of realty for individual ownership today, and 2. an understanding of the impact of exploding populations on the employment, development, financing, transfer, and taxation of land in civilized countries.

Access to Land

It is useless to talk about investing in real estate or related securities unless privately-owned land is permitted within the economy of the country in question. For instance, it is witless to consider personal or corporate real estate investment in Soviet Russia or Communist China because all the land in these nations is government-owned. You may read about a Russian official basking in the luxury of a dachau on the Black Sea. But it should be noted that: 1. the Red official doesn't own the land, 2. he probably built it "on the Q.T." with sneaked-in capital or penal labor, and 3. got the wood, bricks, plumbing, etc. for it by slinky bureaucratic intrigues.

Further, if the official enjoying the equivalent of a Palm Beach mansion offends any of the "top cats" in government and falls from power, his dachau will swiftly acquire a new occupant!

There is even the question in Russia as to actual title to furniture, T.V. sets, cars, and motor bikes, which people use as their own. Where could people store them if they became political black sheep? In an apartment or house? No, because they don't own any. In a public warehouse? If the government blacklisted them they couldn't even store mothballs there!

In both Russia and China there are great agricultural communes, but no individuals own them; and as a tenant farmer in either of these countries the best you could hope to get is a percentage of crop or livestock realizations, at rates set by the agents or commissars. The capital for purchasing sophisticated farm machinery or increasing quality and quantity of product is all supplied, rationed, granted, or denied by government. Thus, no Russians ever become real estate tycoons or land millionaires.

In most of the countries of the Free World, however, there is generally adequate access to land by resourceful individuals. It's tough in Indian states, where supposedly no one, can own more than 30 acres; but those in India who are politically sophisticated manage to find ways around that.

In Argentina, Chile, and Brazil great landowners own thousands of ranch acres. Realty ownership is available to other citizens, but because most of them are poor, property ownership, though permitted, is rare. Each new liberal political regime in these countries as also in Peru, Ecuador, Columbia, and Costa Rica, plumps solidly for a more equitable distribution of land among the peasants and laborers. Foreigners, however, have been able to buy realty in many South American countries. In the 1950s, for example, raw and remote land could have been bought in British Honduras, Costa Rica, Venezuela, and Brazil for $1 to $3 an acre.

Regardless of freedom of access to land, governments (or government subdivisions) own most of the land in many nations. Even in the United States, where land and home ownership represent a way of life, the government (or states) still owns 30 percent of all of the land! Of course, the best located and most desirable metropolitan, industrial, suburban, waterside, farm, and mining land areas are privately owned. The government still retains title to great stretches of parks, deserts, forests and mountain land, not yet released under railway, homestake, mining, or timber grants.

In the United States, land and structures are easily available to all who have the needed money and the acquisitive desire. Most people, however, like their real property managed by others, so there have come into existence thousands of corporations and realty trusts to own, build on, lease, improve, mortgage, sell, leaseback and operate property—all the way from farm, timber or grazing land to clusters of hotels, high-rise apartments, shopping centers, and skyscrapers. It is the ownership of realty by stock or trust certificate and the benefits, tax shelters, capital gains, and dependable income to be realized there from, that is the subject of this book: in other words, how to possess real estate and prosper with it while delegating most of its management and maintenance burdens to others.

We plan to unfold our topic in a progression—from the raw land through to liens on and equity in the most modern and expensive urban buildings—chapter by chapter.

CHAPTER II

Raw Land and Its Potential Upgrading in Use and Price

IN our description of the opportunities for investing in real property and mortgages via negotiable certificates, we should first consider how much land remains that is remote, undeveloped, unused, and not on the market. About 30 percent of the entire land area of the United States is still owned (1968) by the Federal Government. Of the 755.4 million acres of Federal land, 470.4 million acres (62 percent) are under Bureau of Land Management; 186.9 million acres (25 percent) under Forest Service; 30.7 million acres under Department of Defense, 26.6 million under Fish and Wild Life Service; 23.3 million, National Park Service and 17.5 million under other Federal agencies. In addition to these huge acreages of vacant land there are millions more owned by states and cities, set aside for parks, reservoirs, timber, and recreational purposes.

To meet the space needs of an expanding population, the government may, in due course, release some of this acreage for homesteading, as was done originally in Oklahoma, Arizona, and New Mexico. Much of this land, however, is so remote, mountainous, arid, erose, or overgrown that it may not be populated or built on for centuries; although on some of it timber, mineral, or petroleum rights may be granted to non-governmental agencies. Right now 70 percent of our population lives on one percent of the land!

In Canada the wide open spaces are still vaster because: 1. Canada's land area is 20 percent larger than the United States, and 2. practically the entire population of the Dominion lives within 150 miles of the American border. The sprawling terrain to the north is tenanted principally by moose, beaver, caribou, bear, mineral prospectors, and mining and lumber camps. Also, in Canada, while individuals and corporations can readily own real estate on most of the land, publicly- or privately-held, the Dominion retains the mineral rights. This practice does not prevail in the United States where, especially in the oil regions of Texas, Louisiana, Oklahoma, and California, tens of thousands of farmers and ranchers have grown rich while retaining their full ownership, by collecting additional 12½ percent royalties from oil produced on their properties.

In the nineteenth century, the U. S. government granted millions of acres of land to railroad companies, partly for rights of way, but more specifically to stimulate the building of rail lines, to open up the country, expand its agricultural industry, and develop trade. These stretches of open land did not seem important at the time, but they proved to be immensely valuable assets when sections of it turned out to be downtown St. Louis, Midtown New York, or suburban Los Angeles. In fact, the possession and gradual upgrading of thousands of acres of raw land has kept several railroads alive and contributed significantly to railway company earnings; and to dividends and capital gains for their shareholders.

Some railroads spun-off their land holdings into separate companies and distributed shares in these to their shareholders. The most famous instance of this was in the case of the Texas and Pacific Railroad. To encourage the building of this line across Texas, the T & P was given 1,971,231 acres of land. At the time, this acreage was barren, unused or given over to cattle grazing (the returns from land devoted to cattle grazing are not usually impressive). Only a small part of these grants was actually needed for rights of way. The rest was "velvet" and became immensely valuable as oil wells were drilled over wide areas. The spun-off unit, Texas & Pacific Land Trust, rewarded T & P stockholders far more than the railroad ever did. Texas & Pacific Land Trust certificates, originally outstanding, sold as high as $10,000 per share in 1926, were then split 100 for one.

Alico Land Co. was similarly formed to take over most of the land holdings of Atlantic Coastline Railroad, and its shares were also spun-off to the railway stockholders. There are now (1970) 2,647,781 shares of Alico outstanding representing ownership of 209,952 acres of Florida land. This has not been extensively improved. More than half of it is in slash pine and other timber, 65,000 acres in pasture, 6465 in citrus orchards, 19,835 in agriculture, and 8689 in miscellaneous uses. Practically speaking, this is nearly all raw land, and stockholders in Alico are potentially waiting to see some of it get mapped up as suburban land worth several thousand dollars an acre as a shopping center; instead of a few hundred as farm or timber land.

The cases of Texas and Pacific and Atlantic Coast Line relate two fundamental progressions associated with realty investment: the constantly upgraded use of land in modern nations, and the almost automatic increase in value as improvements are made, and as people in increasing numbers move onto the land. Even though land today may be remote from any city or town with no access highways, rivers, or railways, it can still be reached by helicopter, explored for minerals, and gain greatly in value if any are found.

Waterside Property

Gains in realty values will vary greatly depending on the nature and location of the land. Throughout history, the land most eagerly sought, occupied and improved upon by man was property located on or near a river, lake, bay, or ocean. This was quite natural. Land in river valleys is always the most fertile, and in earlier civilizations farming was the most important occupation. The proverbial "cradles of civilization" —and the first real estate booms—were all on the banks and flatlands of the Nile, the Tigris and Euphrates, the Yangtse, and the Ganges. The fertility of river and delta regions attracted settlers, provided food for larger population, and boosted land values. Waterside locations on navigable rivers and in naturally sheltered harbors were given top valuations, as man began to engage in commerce and to learn and perfect the art of naval warfare. Thus, most of the famous port cities such as Tyre, Sidon, Antioch, Corinth, Alexandria, Ephesus, Genoa, Florence, Marseilles, Hong Kong, and Singapore, became major centers of trade and population, and their land values soared. In the United States, explosive expansions in population, productivity, commerce, and land prices emanated from its seaport cities: New York, Boston, Philadelphia, Savannah, New Orleans, San Francisco, Seattle, and inland waterway ports such as Pittsburgh, St. Louis, Chicago, Detroit, Cleveland, and Minneapolis.

Whether for agriculture or commerce, or the recreations of boating, swimming, or fishing, land located near the water has usually commanded higher prices than inland acreage. Homes facing the water command the highest values in California, Florida, and in all of those areas where land development has been most energetic. In Florida, entire communities have been built around dredged-out lagoons and man-made canals, in order that homeowners can have a power boat moored on their property. Such land is usually worth 30 percent to 40 percent more than sites in the same area, away from the water.

We have gone out of our way to dwell on this waterside concept, because you will find it important as an investment consideration. As we describe residential land development

securities in a later chapter, you may note the effect on earning power of those companies that have accented waterfront
locations as they have converted raw acreage into modern
home or retirement communities.

Relatively slow transportation by water and by land
(horse, camel, and donkey) until the nineteenth century
tended to make inland communities and regions unattractive
to investors and slow to expand because so much time was
required to reach them from metropolitan centers. The railroads did much to change that. In fact, many an inland city
today owes its progress and major growth to the fact that a
railroad company decided (or was persuaded) to run its
tracks through it.

In the past fifty years the amazing growth in motor cars
and highway transportation, the current delivery of 20 percent of our intercity freight by truck, plus jet air travel, have
broken down time and distance barriers. What was once a
sleepy town 40 miles from a metropolis, is now a bustling
exurban community awash with $50,000 homes—and land
values that have rocketed 500 percent to 1,000 percent due to
accessibility.

These factors—near water location and access to modern
transportation—are important determinants in the value of
real estate. Often you will note that a company has bought
acreage in an undeveloped area and you may wonder why. It
may be because the management suspected, or had special
knowledge of, a new highway or airport to be built nearby.
If such improvements were made then the company land
would swiftly appreciate in market price, and blossom into a
motel or shopping center with significant earning power.

The main idea to keep in mind as you search for rewarding
corporate realty investments is that in general, land prices are
the resultants of population. As more people come on a given
section of land, whether to build homes, to work in stores,
office buildings, factories, financial institutions, or super-

markets, they create a demand for living space, land and structures. This demand, except during a depression, seems likely to expand indefinitely. A sustained rise in realty prices over the next century is perhaps the most predictable of all economic possibilities.

The arrival of people (except in ghetto areas), upgrades land and works constantly toward its maximum use. From your own personal experience, you know this to be so. In any city with a population of 500,000 or more with which you are familiar, you have seen something like this happen. In a section of the city, only a mile or two from the major downtown business hub, there was quite probably between 1945-1955 a vacant lot, perhaps 200 feet by 300 feet. In 1950, the same area might have sported a couple of tennis courts where business men played during their lunch hour or after work, paying $5 to $10 an hour rental for the privilege.

Soon this revenue became inadequate for so valuable a plot. The tennis nets and backstops were torn down and the space converted to a parking lot charging $2 or $3 a day per car, thus increasing the income.

The next step might have been discontinuance of the parking lot and the building of a two-story "taxpayer" housing perhaps an insurance agency, attorneys' offices, a lunch counter, or a business machine rental service and a travel agency. That again expanded the revenue from the property, and added 200 percent or 300 percent to the value of the underlying land.

The next step, probably in the 1960s, was the ultimate one resulting from the pressures of business and people on a choice land area. Around this 200 feet by 300 feet lot, new buildings had already been built: two office buildings, a bank, an insurance company home office, a postal branch, and a Montgomery Ward store. These buildings and the people at work in them exerted powerful pressure to place all nearby land in equally productive use because: 1. there was a need for new and enlarged facilities, and 2. the taxes on the land had so increased that the only way to offset them was to build a larger structure capable of generating increased revenues. Thus by 1970, on this land vacant only 25 years earlier, there now stands a modern 20-story office building that cost $10 million to build.

The land on which this architectural gem stands (which sold for $1 million in 1945), is now worth $3 million. The taxes paid to the city on the empty lot were $30,000 a year in 1945; while today the annual realty tax on land and building is $220,000. In similar ways, people are constantly enhancing realty values all over the world—serving economic needs and making fortunes for the perceptive early investors (corporate or individual), and improvers of land.

The upward trend in suburban real estate values is not usually at as rapid a rate as downtown or midtown commercially-oriented property, but the principle is still the same— people push up prices!

To illustrate further, broad stretches of land on Long Island, 20 miles east of New York City and farther out, right after World War II were devoted principally to growing potatoes and cabbages. As farmland it was worth variously from $150 to $250 an acre; and nobody was clamoring for it. From 1945 on, however, the population push in the New York area and the postwar move to the suburbs caused thousands of homes to be built on Long Island in a wide belt extending from Roslyn, Hempstead, and Rockville Center, east to Locust Valley, Plainview, Huntington, Smithtown, and Babylon. Land prices soared, going to $3,000 and $5,000 an acre for homes, and $50,000 to $100,000 an acre for motels, department stores, and shopping centers built along new highways and cross-island arteries.

Upgrading here meant taking a flat potato field, subdividing it into building lots, putting in streets, sidewalks, curbs, drainage, water, and electricity; and then dotting the area with thousands of homes and building the requisite and related schools, fire houses, police stations, and parks. In most of this Long Island grid, raw land prices rose from 1000 percent to 3000 percent between 1945 and 1970; and a house on 100 feet by 100 feet property costing $15,000 in 1945 brought $35,000 or more, 25 years later.

This sort of price progression was duplicated in most metropolitan suburban areas across the land; Cleveland, Hartford, Boston, Birmingham, Charlotte, Atlanta, Orlando, Dallas, Denver, Milwaukee, Los Angeles, San Francisco, Seattle, and Phoenix. It is still going on in an everwidening exurban circle. The Hamptons on Long Island and the country 25 miles outside Denver, for example, are now in the same kind of realty upcurve as the suburban upswing described earlier.

In land more remotely situated from where the people are, the upcurve is far slower; although in relatively unpopulated sections of Vermont and New Hampshire, land going begging a decade ago at $50 or $100 an acre is being snapped up for recreation or retirement housing at several hundred dollars an acre; and land in the fashionable ski country around Manchester, Vermont, may fetch as much as $3,500 an acre, if it's on or near a main highway.

Raw land, miles and possibly decades away from becoming a town suburb, parking lot, or golf course, while less in demand, benefits price wise as more attractive and accessible acreage is no longer available at reasonable prices.

In fact the only acreages in America not potentially on a price upcurve are worked-out farms on the prairies and the "Dust Bowl"; desert, and stripped-out and devastated land in West Virginia and Kentucky; city slums, swampland and marshes. Even these tired terrains are not hopeless. They might someday yield up valuable oil or minerals. You can't even count out desert land. Look what they did to arid cactus pastures outside of Phoenix, Arizona. Acres in Scottsdale worth no more than $1.00 a quarter century ago now bring $3,000 and more. "The desert shall blossom like a rose!"

The most likely sources of an increased value on wild,

mountainous, remote, irregular, and unsettled land are timber, furs, pasturage, petroleum, and minerals. Later on we'll
cite some specific companies wherein substantial revenues
from these natural resources are being realized or in prospect.
With the variety of modern vehicles available—helicopters,
tractors, half tracks, bulldozers, amphibians and snow
mobiles—no land is remote any more. Billions of barrels of
oil were found beneath the frozen wastes of the Arctic in 1969.
And no area is more forbidding than that! The potential
mineral yields from acreages "out in the wilds" can now be
rather accurately estimated by use of magnetometers and
other sophisticated instruments. Even mountaintops or moose
pastures may shelter rich stores of copper, uranium, lead,
zinc, nickel, silver, gold, asbestos, oil, or natural gas. You
might well argue that no land is worthless; and you might
even perceive wisdom in the statement of the old Arkansas
farmer out in the razor-back country who, when asked by a
stranger "What good is your land?" replied, "Well, it helps
hold the world together!"

All real estate was once vacant land; so keep in mind its
underlying importance as you read about the dozens of companies we shall evaluate as possible rewarding and gainful
real estate investments.

CHAPTER III

Land Development Companies

THERE are approximately 30 publicly-held companies with sizeable holdings of unimproved land planned, or suitable, for residential or resort development. Of these, perhaps 20 are generating a large or major portion of their net incomes through installment sale of land projects. A review of such companies and their operations quite logically follows the subject of raw land treated in Chapter II.

Perhaps the best known converter of acreage into homes is the Levitt Development Corporation, now a division of International Telephone and Telegraph. The Levitt name is renowned for Levittown, a community of thousands of homes developed from scratch on suburban Long Island, and a similar development on the Delaware River near Philadelphia. Levitt was a pioneer in the assembly and improvement of land acreage and construction in volume of modest-priced houses to create modern home communities. Levitt, under the ITT aegis, continues as a leader in this field; but because its divisional contribution to the parent corporation earnings is small in relation to the total, we shall concentrate on other companies where land development is a more significant factor in earning power.

Most people have a rather vague idea about land project companies. They seem to believe that all such an enterprise needs to do is pick up a swath of land at wholesale prices, touch it up a little, and sell it for swift capital gains. In practice, the increase in land prices and the gleaning of juicy profits is not all that easy!

A good land project company must have: 1. substantial capital, 2. a management experienced in land development and building construction, 3. a shrewd eye for regions that are attractive or strategically located for future population expansion, 4. strong sales capability, and 5. financial expertise in the arranging and handling of installment contracts, bank and institutional loans, mortgages and equity financing. For sales growth at a desired rate of 20 percent or more annually, it is essential that there be plenty of capital available and a rather broad-based marketing organization.

The general operational procedure is like this. A company decides that Florida is likely to continue among the fastest growing states in the nation during the 1970 decade. It looks around to find a stretch of 50,000 acres available on the market, which it acquires in due course at an assumed price of $125 an acre. It all starts from there.

The land thus acquired is carefully mapped out, the location of roads decided on, lots are plotted and the project assumes shape. The area must be graded and drained, roads must be put in, and in some developments water mains and sewer pipes. Land in its raw state is never fit for building and the developers will spend from 12 percent to 18 percent of the ultimate sales price of the land on these essential improvements.

When the land is ready, a sales brochure is prepared portraying the desirability of owning a building lot at "Elysian Acres." It not only shows a panorama of the land, but the different types and costs of homes that may be built on it. Then the sales force takes over. Only 20 percent of the lots will be sold to Florida residents. Most of the lots will be sold in the cities of the North. Accordingly, the company will have an office or representatives in such cities as New York, Chicago, Detroit, Minneapolis, Cleveland, or Boston. The land is sold on commission. Franchised dealers will receive commissions ranging between 15 percent to 25 percent of homesites (and 3 percent to 10 percent on houses sold). Salesmen are paid commissions of between 5 percent and 10 percent on homesites sales.

Method of Sale

There are very few sales for cash and almost all of the business is done on installments. Typical contract is 5 percent down and the balance to be paid in equal monthly installments over a 7 to 9 year period, with interest at 6 percent. Somewhere from 5 percent to 15 percent of sales in a current year, and perhaps 5 percent to 10 percent of sales made in earlier years, will be cancelled. These, of course, represent additional costs incurred by the land project company. This business is not all "clover!"

In accounting for a sale, the distribution would look something like this:

Homesite Sales Price	—	$2,500
Cash Deposit	$ 125	
Contract Receivable	2,325	
	$2,500	

Against this ultimate realization would be charged:

Cost of Sales	$ 500.00
Commission	125.00
Land	125.00
Estimated Cost of Improvement	400.00
Allowance for Cancellation	125.00
	$1,275.00

The difference between the $2,500 sale, and the $1,275 sale in total costs, plus interest income on the installment balance, roughly represents the theoretical gross profit realized by the company. But it doesn't stop there. As we mentioned earlier, the eternal propulsion for higher land price is "people coming on the property."

In the 50,000-acre project we have outlined, sale of land and the increased building on it are enhancing factors. As improved land is sold and the project is rounded out by a community recreational and civic center (pools, playgrounds, shuffleboard, etc.), houses of worship, on-site or adjacent banks, and shopping centers, something quite predictable happens. The homesites are no longer worth $2,500 but perhaps $3,000 or $3,500, and the land company at the end of three or four years of sales may wind up still owning 10,000 acres costing originally $125 per acre and, after improvements, $575 an acre which can now be sold at a 400 percent gain!

This is the overspin—the extra profitability—in land development companies, that by the very process of upgrading the land and bringing hundreds of new owners on the property, the sum of the parts is greater than the original "whole." The enhancement of land values is further promoted by the quality and caliber of houses built on the sites. A number of land companies—Deltona, Great American Land, Gulf American Corp. (GAC), Amrep, Horizon Land—derive an increasing amount of total sales from actual building of homes for those who have bought the land. For example, Deltona Corp. housing sales are close to $18 million, or about 18 percent of total annual revenues of $98 million (1969). This home building may be expected to be an increasing percentage of land companies sales in the future. As mortgage money becomes more available (it was very tight in 1970), and improved building technology emerges (pre-manufactured housing and modular construction), the major trend may swing away from individual home construction to multi-family units, to garden apartments, and condominiums.

The type of housing development is tailored to the kind of buyer solicited. For example, the price of a General Development home completed in 1969 ran between $16,000 and $20,000; while the average price of a Marco (Florida) home, developed by Deltona would have been about $36,000. The lower-priced home (up to $20,000) can be financed by F.H.A., while the higher-priced units depend for mortgage financing on banks, financial institutions and savings and loan associations.

While there are five or six major public companies in this area that represent especially interesting values, we have selected one of the largest and perhaps the most quality oriented as a corporate example—Deltona Corporation. As of June 30, 1969, this company had a total inventory of 31,400 acres and an "inventory" of about 60,700 "lots." The selling prices of the lots in 1969 were approximately $2,000 in Citrus Country; $2,900 at Deltona, and around $11,000 at Marco Island (where $36,000 homes are being built).

Up to September 30, 1969, Deltona had reported total land sales of $180 million and had spent $25 million for land development. Uniquely in the industry, Deltona plans to install water mains for all its homesites. In the five years ended December 31, 1969, Deltona increased its sales a little better than 30 percent annually. At Deltona, selling and administrative expense run annually about 30 percent of sales; provision for cancellations 9.5 percent; total corporate interest 4.9 percent, and gross profit margin on land sales roughly 64 percent. Deltona spent about $4 million on improvements in 1969. As of June 30, 1969, a projection of future sales value of land (after improvement) from its inventories and major developments in progress might have been, very roughly, $525 million.

Installment land companies are something like life insurance companies in that all expenses connected with homesite sales are customarily charged against income after sale has been made. These expenses include the average cost of the unimproved land, capitalized interest, mortgage, and real estate taxes. Land companies use accrual accounting for their financial reports and the installment method (deferring profits) for Internal Revenue reporting. This results in substantial sums in deferred taxes (payable as installments due which are collected in later years). In September, 1969, Deltona had a deferred tax liability of about $16½ million (For Gulf American, the tax deferral total at that time would have been approximately $62 million.)

This dual method of accounting will probably be continued as long as companies conservatively provide for cancellations and make full charges for land development costs. The favorable results in recent years reported by Deltona and several other companies might not continue if we were to have a serious depression which would reduce land prices, slow down sales, and drastically increase the prevailing percentages of contract cancellations.

Nearly all real estate ventures are highly leveraged, in the belief that well-located land is likely to increase over a period of time. Deltona is a highly-leveraged company with (September 30, 1969) about $63 million in long-term debt, out of a total capitalization of $94 million.

As companies expand and make appropriate additions to their land inventory, they need increasing amounts of capital; therefore several installment land companies will be doing major financing in the 1970s. The nature of the business generates a negative cash flow until the volume of annual installment payments and the interest on it has built up substantially. This negative cash flow is the result of the large percentage of sales revenues paid out each year in sales commissions, promotional, general, and administrative expenses; and the interest charges on high leveraged capitalizations. Even large companies such as Deltona and General Development, until 1970 had not reached positive cash flows from land operations.

Other interesting land development companies are NOR-TEK Inc., developing 43,000 acres in 15 areas in Florida;

Centex Corporation of Dallas, a large homebuilding and construction firm that in early 1971 purchased the 38-acre site of Palisades Amusement Park, near the New Jersey terminus of the George Washington Bridge opposite uptown New York; and Co-Build Companies, Inc., the major land developer of the Virgin Islands with an important waterside community development in lower New Jersey as well; and McCulloch Oil Corp., a petroleum company with a large scale land development in Arizona; and General Builders Corp., a developer of condominiums in Florida.

Smaller home developers would include Disc Inc., in Washington, D.C., and Pickwick Organization, Inc. of Huntington, Long Island.

Summary

The factors favoring land project companies are: 1. expected correction of the cumulative lag in housing built up during 1968–70, 2. prediction of a rise of $3,500 in disposable per-family income by 1980, 3. the sustained attraction of Florida, the middle South and the Southwestern regions as havens for the retired, 4. the continuing inflationary trend, 5. disenchantment with the equity markets of 1969–70, creating preference for real estate as a long-term investment, 6. the costs of construction labor are rising about 15 percent annually, so that a house built today should be worth more two years hence, if ony because of the higher cost to duplicate it.

No doubt competition will increase in this field, as great corporations such as I.T. & T., Kaiser-Aetna, and Ford Motor Company apply their large resources and technical competencies to mass market residential building. It is most important, however, that a land company, regardless of its size, deliver land to the contracting buyer improved as promised and on schedule. Equally, contracts for houses built on homesites must be scrupulously completed.

Keeping these points in mind, you now have a background

for evaluating land company equities, and reasonable expectations for gleaning capital gains in the 1970s, if you select the right stock. Get the latest annual report on the companies that interest you, consult the opinion of your broker or financial advisor, and get a report from one of the investment services. Look for such key statistics as capital leverage ratios, cancellation rates, sales costs, and annual interest charges. Inquire too about the character and quality of homes being built by company developments. And prefer companies whose net profits are steadily increasing.

Homes of better quality in such things as construction, plumbing, and landscaping, enhance the value of residual land retained, or sold last, by the developer. A land boom in a given region can rocket the capital gains potential of a company sitting on the "right" land tract. Also, as land companies prosper, their stocks will perform like other glamor-type equities and increase their price/earnings multiples even faster than earnings increase.

Land companies can become speculative favorites in the right kind of market climate. Look for good managements, strong balance sheets, and strategic land spreads.

CHAPTER IV

Real Estate Values in Railroad Stocks

THE continuing inflation which we face in America is both stimulating and broadening the investor interest in real estate. Significant participation in realty is possible not only through investment in the securities of realty, mortgages, and hotel-motel companies and realty trusts, but indirectly through share ownership in forest product, mineral, petroleum, and railway companies whose assets often include substantial ownership of raw and improved land. In this chapter we are looking at some well-known American railroads selected because of their historic overtones in real estate.

How did the railways wind up owning so much land? They were granted land outright, either by states or the Federal Government, not only for rights-of-way but to have available sites for commerce and industry along the tracks to assure future growth of sizeable communities in the regions they served. As a consequence of a national business and political climate favorable to railway building, a whole series of lines —Texas & Pacific, Southern Pacific, Union Pacific, Burlington-Great Northern, and Canadian Pacific—all were granted substantial acreages quite early in their corporate lives.

Railroads also bought land, usually alongside of or adjacent to their rights-of-way, for freight or switching yards, terminals, warehouses, or industrial sites to locate freight-producing companies on their lines, or to build (in earlier years), hotels or office buildings. The Delaware & Hudson for years owned hotels on Lake Champlain and Lake George; the Chesapeake & Ohio owned convention and resort hotels; and the New York Central (now a part of troubled Penn Central), still owns land on which many splendid Park Avenue hotels and office buildings now stand.

More recently, railways have bought real estate companies as part of a long-range program of diversification. The purchase of controlling interests in Great Southwest Corp. and Arvida Corporation by Penn Central (however unwise or ill-timed), illustrates this type of realty acquisition.

Regardless of how these properties and various realty tracts came into the fold it is a fact that today those rail stocks that appear to have the most spirited investor followings are ones with a good chunk of real estate "going for them"—either as earning assets or as hostages-to-fortune in years ahead in the form of farm, grazing, mineral-prone, fruit or timber-bearing acreages. There are no standard rules or criteria for the selection of rail stocks on the basis of their land assets. Each carrier is a case unto itself with respect to total extent, kind or valuation, land uses and revenue sources developed, and land possibilities for future gains in market value and annual income. Accordingly, to develop our theme and to highlight certain relationships between railway realty holdings and share valuations, we'll take a quick look at several representative railways.

Canadian Pacific

One of the great railway properties in the world is Canadian Pacific. Its assets and sources of earnings are so diversified that the company might easily qualify as a complete investment trust in its own right. It owns, in addition to a 16,600-mile transcontinental railway extending from St. John, New Brunswick, on the Atlantic to Vancouver, British Columbia, on the Pacific, Canadian Pacific Air Lines, Ltd.

(6000 miles of domestic air and freight routes and 50,000 global route miles over five continents); Canadian Pacific Steamships, Ltd. and Canadian Pacific Bermuda, Ltd., operators of passenger and cargo vessels; and three subsidiary trucking companies.

Non-transportation interests of C. P. are consolidated in Canadian Pacific Investments, Ltd., a holding company formed in 1962. Affiliated within this huge holding company are: a 53 percent interest in Cominco, Ltd., with substantial holdings of mineral land and a large producer of metals, chemicals and fertilizers; 9 percent of Panarctic Oils, Ltd., controlling oil and gas rights on some 50 million Arctic Island acres; interests in other oil companies; Pacific Logging, Ltd., with timberland holdings; C. P. Hotels, Ltd., and Marathon Realty Co., owner of extensive hotel, commercial and industrial properties, including the Royal York in Toronto and the Queen Elizabeth in Montreal.

C. P. Investments already has underway a program for constructing a three-block midtown complex in Montreal to embrace three office tower buildings, a high-rise apartment structure, a hotel and a new railroad depot. You should get the latest C. P. Annual Report for a full catalog of its land holdings—including millions of acres of timber and mineral land—the largest cluster of land assets possessed by any railroad.

Union Pacific Corp.

This holding company was formed in 1969 to broaden the business horizons and to facilitate the expansion of one of the most renowned American transportation companies—Union Pacific Railroad—with 9500 miles of track running from the Missouri River to the Pacific Coast. This railroad has paid continuous dividends since 1900, and consistently evidenced managerial competence in depth.

While railway operations, now conducted through the Transportation Division, are still the major revenue producers, the Land Division of UNP generates plenty of romance and rising annual profits. The road owns the rights on approximately 7.85 million acres of land spread over 13 Western states. Of this, UNP owns coal rights on 270,000 acres, all mineral rights on 6.63 million acres, and both the land and mineral rights on 950,000 acres. In addition, UNP owns 17,300 acres useful as possible industrial sites along its lines, and for residential and commercial development in the Salt Lake City region, and around Las Vegas and in Southern California. The lands include producing oil fields in Colorado, Wyoming, and California, and low sulphur coal reserves now being extensively and profitably mined. Added to these are the realty possessions of Champlain Petroleum Corp. and Pontiac Refining, acquired in 1969.

UNP common earning about $4 a share in 1970 and paying a reliable $2.00 dividend, is outstanding in the amount of 21,120,000 shares. The stock sold as high as 64 in 1969. It combines the solid earning power of the railway with the interesting facets of expanding earning power from oil, coal, and industrial, commercial, and residential properties, and the steady upgrading of the company's raw land.

Southern Pacific

Much like Union Pacific Corp., Southern Pacific Company was formed in 1969 to combine under one roof, the railroad operating 14,000 miles of track from Illinois and Louisiana to the West Coast, pipeline, and trucking operations, and large land and natural resource holdings.

The realty includes the routing of a wholly-owned petroleum transportation network of 2438 miles, the Southern Pacific Pipe Lines. Much of this pipeline mileage runs underneath or beside the railroad tracks. Far more important in the realty category are the 3.8 million acres of land owned by SX, but not used in transportation. Of these, 2 million acres are in California and 1.6 million in Nevada—suitable in the years ahead for urban and industrial development. Also, SX has the oil, gas, and mineral rights on 1.3 million acres—plus 33,000 acres strategically situated for ultimate industrial use and the attraction of new shippers along the railroad rights of way.

Currently, SX common pays $1.80, with earnings of around $3.30 a share. The 26,935,000,000 shares outstanding sold as high as 50 in 1968. It is another seasoned vehicle for playing rails and realty back-to-back.

Southern Railway

This East and Southeastern carrier is a very well-run railroad, but lacks the broad land play found in UNP or SX. Southern's land assets consist of about 20,000 acres of rather high-priced land, well located for industrial use close to the rail lines.

St. Louis San Francisco Railway Company

This railway has realty overtones through its ownership of 51 percent of New Mexico & Arizona Land Co., with some 800,000 acres of land in those two states. A better way to share in the realty of FN (Stock Exchange Symbol for St. Louis San Francisco), is to purchase directly the shares of New Mexico and Arizona Land trading on AMEX.

Santa Fe Industries

This holding company for the famous 13,000 mile Atchison Topeka and Sante Fe Railroad, finds its representation in real estate through Kirby Lumber Co., 94 percent owned, which produces timber and plywood from its 594,000 acres of woodland in Texas and Louisiana; and from the Santa Fe Improvement Company, developing industrial property in the railroads operating territory.

Florida East Coast

Perhaps half of the valuation of Florida East Coast common (selling as this was written at 24), is attributed to its ownership of land standing on the books at about $5 million, but believed to be worth at "going" prices in 1970 between $75 and $100 million. This land is not swamp, pasture, or citrus land, but made up of strategically located industrial lands including about: 1250 acres in the Jacksonville area, 300 in St. Augustine, and 200 acres each in Fort Pierce and New Smyrna; a total of several hundred acres in Del Ray, Lake Worth, West Palm Beach; four industrial parks totaling 260 acres; 400 acres in Miami, including 26 very valuable commercial waterfront and dock properties; and 320 acres near the Hialeah Yard.

All of this and 554 miles of probably the most efficiently operated railway in America belongs to the owners of 1,453,-000 shares of Florida East Coast common. Long-term debt is below $19.5 million.

Burlington Northern, Inc.

Another big land owner is Burlington Northern, Inc., formed by the 1970 merger of Northern Pacific and Great Northern Railway, and their jointly owned subsidiaries— Chicago, Burlington and Quincy, and the Spokane Portland and Seattle RR—some 26,500 miles of railroad in total. Other partners had some good real estate, but Northern Pacific brought along 2.2 million acres of land owned in fee (about half in commercial forest land) and mineral rights on an additional 6 million acres—much of it in the renowned

Williston Basin Oil Fields real estate generated revenues—oil, gas, timber and realty rents—produced $46.6 million in 1969.

Western Railroads

Other Western roads—the Rock Island, Denver & Rio Grande Western, and Western Pacific—lack real estate holdings of such size as to produce revenues or realty earnings that significantly affect the value of their common stocks. Norfolk & Western owns real estate, but its only really significant holdings are in coal land.

From this swift and "broad-brush" picture of railway land holdings, you can form some conclusions as to which are the more attractive and potentially rewarding to landowners. A number of the common stocks of these lines pay generous cash dividends and provide above average yields. These returns, high book values, and in some cases, interesting potentials for expanded net worth via land assets, may suggest investment in railway stocks when "the price is right!"

We did not include Penn Central in the active list, because although land holdings are great, they are heavily mortgaged, appear to have been poorly managed, and the values they may ultimate create are clouded by the bankruptcy and tragic shortage of working capital of the Penn Central Transportation Company, the railway operating subsidiary of the Penn Central Company.

CHAPTER V

Office Building Specialists

A survey of publicly-held companies that build and/or own and operate urban commercial buildings, together with some observations on trends in this sector of the real estate market.

OFFICE buildings have long ranked among the choicest, most desirable, and most prestigious realty investments. Only in recent years, however, has it been possible for the public to own stock in them, because the business historically has been almost entirely confined to and controlled by wealthy families, private syndicates, financial institutions, and corporations with their own office buildings.

The significant families in urban real estate are fairly well known: the Goelets, the Rhinelanders, the Rockefellers, the Kennedys, the Astors; syndicate members such as Colonel Crown of Chicago, Lawrence Wien, and H. Helmsley of New York; and a group of New York families who early in this century staked out major careers in the construction of, and investment in, office buildings—the Fishers, Dursts, Minskoffs, Tishmans, Urises, Kaufmans, Roses, and Rudins. Some of these families and their holdings are now identified with public companies, but all of them got their start and gained great resources and stature as variously, private builders, owners, and operators.

Office Buildings

The skyscraper has stimulated the enthusiasm and imagination of businessmen, bankers, architects, and institutions. The early skyscrapers, such as the Flatiron Building and the Woolworth Building in New York, were tourist attractions until the 1920s, when dozens of new buildings towered up, dwarfing in size and altitude these earlier landmarks. Second generation skyscrapers included the Chrysler Building and the Empire State Building in New York, both completed and yawning for occupants as the Depression deepened in 1932. Later in the 1930s, the huge complex of lofty commercial structures in Radio City was built, followed by dozens of great structures on Third and Park Avenues, north of 42nd. Street, flowering in the Pan American and Seagram Buildings in the 1960s, and the General Motors Building on Fifth Avenue at the end of the decade.

A similar dedication to massive altitudinous structures was in evidence in all the major metropolitan centers—Chicago, Dallas, Houston, Minneapolis, Seattle, Los Angeles, San Francisco, Boston, Detroit, Miami, Atlanta, Washington, and St. Louis.

The boom in office buildings during 1960 was by far the largest in history. In 1967, 6.6 million new square feet of office space came on-stream in New York City; 8.8 million additional square feet in 1968; 10 million in 1969; 11 million in 1970; and some 28 million square feet of new space (including the new twin 100-story Trade Center Buildings) which will be available for occupancy in 1971. It appears, however, while this was being written (December 1970) that, as occurred in 1933 and again in 1962, office space has been overbuilt, temporarily at least. During 1970, office space rentals in New York City fell off by as much as 15 percent, and by December 1, 1970, 8 percent of office space was vacant throughout the city, against less than one percent two years earlier. In Chicago, rentals had fallen by 12 percent; and around 14 percent in Seattle and Los Angeles, where cutbacks in space-age and aviation industries had created a significant contraction in office space required.

This 1970 slack-off in rental, property prices, and occupancies in cities across the nation (except in Houston) brought a halt to a steady long-term market rise in prices of urban commercial buildings, in progress almost without interruption since 1933. The downturn was highlighted by the difficulties of a leading "offshore" mutual fund called Gramco International, owning about 270 metropolitan American buildings (mostly commercial) costing over $800 million.

Gramco got into such a bind that it had to stop redeeming certificates for investors who sought to convert them into cash; and in November 1970 went into a moratorium because it was unable to liquidate property at acceptable prices, and lacked funds to finance two new office buildings in a partnership with Uris Bros. and Arlen properties. Gramco and the liquidating problems of a second and smaller offshore fund, Real Estate Fund of America, certainly slowed down the commercial building boom and led to some reappraisals of the immediate income and gain prospects for urban realty in general.

The long-range economic advantages of owning and operating urban structures, however, remains favorable. First, the leverage is attractive, since for most of the postwar years, it was possible to get long-term mortgages on completed and well-tenanted buildings, of 70 percent to 80 percent of the total building cost. In general practice, an operator would line up an attractive urban site and arrange to either buy it, or build on a long-term leasehold. Then he would sign up tenants, preferably big corporations with triple A credit, to lease several floors for 15 to 20 years (with escalation to cover higher annual costs of labor, taxes and maintenance).

If one big company took enough space, the operator might agree to name the building after it. (Pan Am, U. S. Steel,

Squibb–Beech Nut, Westvaco are examples). Armed with the prime leases assuring dependable and adequate revenues for years to come, the operator/owner could obtain a construction loan of 75 percent of costs, and he was then ready to start excavating. As the building "went up," the operator strove to get additional tenants, hopefully up to 100 percent occupancy, (although 70 percent was usually enough to "break even").

At that point, the investment became a rewarding one. Rentals provided a comfortable income tax sheltered by depreciation on the building. This created a large cash flow and tax benefits making the venture yield well. After substantial and frequently accelerated depreciation had been taken for several years, the property might be sold at a handsome capital gain over its original cost. Then a similar operation could be started all over again. Tending to assure the success of these urban building operations, was the steady advance in urban property values, impelled by expanding population and economic activity; and the increasing scarcity of strategically located "downtown" building sites. Further, the costs of labor and materials have been rising so steadily that most operators have preferred to put up buildings, even ahead of visible demand for space, on the theory that it would cost 8 percent to 10 percent more to construct the same edifice a year later.

Of course, these rises in underlying land prices, plus constantly higher costs of new construction, stimulated a strong market and excellent demand for completed and well-tenanted modern buildings among all kinds of buyers: individuals, syndicates, realty trusts, or realty corporations, financial institutions, and pension funds.

This line of reasoning proved logical and profitable for several decades. The argument has developed a few flaws in the past three years, however. Crime in the big cities, frustrations, costs and delays of transportation, expensive lunching, smog and noise, and concern about trapped tenants in possible fires

(even in ultra-modern "fireproof" buildings); and the beckon-
ing attractions of suburban living, have all dampened somewhat the historic trend toward tenant expansion in huge
metropolitan business towers. In fact, in the past few years,
such big companies as IBM, General Telephone, General
Foods, Shell Oil, and Combustion Engineering have all
shifted their major space from New York office buildings to
suburban centers of their own.

In Hartford, Connecticut General Life Insurance moved
from downtown to a big, suburban headquarters building.
This trend, if continued and accelerated, might in some meas-
ure revise the opinions of sophisticated investors who have
long viewed with favor the income, growth, and gain potentials of downtown office emporia. The answer may be found
in more attractive, homelike, and less cubicle urban office
centers with terraces, landscaping, and perhaps pneumatic-
tube transit to whisk people to suburban residences in a matter of minutes.

Interesting Public Companies

Regardless of the direction of future trends, there are some
very fine public companies deriving substantial income and
creating steadily larger annual cash flows from investment in
modern urban properties of the kind we have been discussing.
These would include Tishman Realty & Construction Co.,
Uris Building Corp., Presidential Realty, Realty Equities
Corp., Pittway Corp., I. C. Industries, Tenneco Corp., New
Plan Realty, Rouse Co., City Investing Co., and the Titan
group.

Tishman Realty

We haven't space here for a detailed description of all of
these companies, but urge that if any particular stock interests

you, you either get from the company itself, from your broker, or an investment advisory or report service, the latest Annual Report and details and current data on properties owned, income, depreciation and cash flow figures, capitalization, growth rate and dividend records.

Tishman Realty and Construction Co., Inc. is a recognized leader in urban development and the only "family" company that is nationwide in its operations. Tishman erects stores, office and apartment buildings in selected cities for its own account and for others. With regard to its own buildings, it either sells them, retains them as investments, or takes them back under long-term leases. Tishman income is derived from its construction operations, interest income, management and operation of properties, rentals and other property income, and capital gains.

As this was written, Tishman was building for its own account, office structures in New York, Chicago, and Los Angeles; and it had, on April 30, 1970, building contracts for others totaling over $1,150,000,000, including major construction in six cities. Tishman's contracting is done for fees ranging between 2 percent and 4 percent of costs. The company was general contractor for the $600 million World Trade Center in New York.

Between 1969 and the end of 1972, Tishman will have added over 4.5 million square feet of urban office space. Tishman has been generally successful in renting its buildings, and finds it preferable to build "this year," carrying the completed property, if necessary, on less than a fully rented basis —rather than to wait and build later at costs escalating at the rate of 8 to 10 percent a year.

Holding and managing its properties over a period of years, building up its cash flow, and potentials for capital gain, are the underlying corporate concepts at Tishman. Asset values have risen steadily. Cash flow, on a per share basis, has enhanced in the five fiscal year period ending September 30,

36 IRA U. COBLEIGH

1970, from $1.03 to $2.13 (in 1970). Current construction should add another $1.25 per share in cash flow by the end of 1974.

Financing

Financing properties is an art in itself. Tishman is very good at this, arranging construction loans at the acceptable rates even under adverse money market conditions. In 1969, a year of high interest rates, Tishman was able to finance its completions at an average rate of 7 percent. In permanent mortgage financing, terms have to be shrewdly negotiated because major lending institutions nowadays frequently seek "a piece of the action"—warrants, or a low priced stock, as a bonus to the customary mortgage interest and amortization provisions. Including lenders in an equity position, while it dilutes the percentage of ownership retained by the construction company, may mean that the property is ultimately 100 percent financed by others; and that the builder will acquire his equity without any outlay of actual cash on his part.

Currently (December, 1970), Tishman owns in fee construction sites in Los Angeles, San Francisco, St. Louis and Alexandria, Virginia, and leaseholds on other sites in New York and Los Angeles, as well as the following structures: three large office buildings and a parking garage in New York, a hotel in Los Angeles, a garage in Chicago, an office building in Cleveland, and a residence hall at Ohio University. Leasebacks included two large office buildings in New York, one each in Cleveland and Buffalo, and six in Los Angeles. In addition, the company held leaseholds on 11 office buildings in various cities; and on a residence hall at the University of Illinois.

Capitalization consists of 5,336,897 shares of common stock, preceded by $205.8 million of mortgages payable. The stock was split 3 for 1 in 1969, and 42 percent is owned by the Tishman family. Dividends have been increased moderately in every year since 1960. Present indicated rate is 40 cents, against per-share-net of $1.10 in fiscal 1970.

Tishman is a leader and a representative company in its field. However, if investment here interests you, you are urged to get information about some of the other companies mentioned above.

If we assume that inflation will be a continuing fact of economic life, that building costs and land prices will continue to increase, and that the custom of major business concentration in urban skyscrapers persists, then a sound case may be made for long-term investment in the stocks of some of these metropolitan developers and property owners. The big realty trusts are avid owners and buyers of office builders; and large corporations such as General Electric, U. S. Steel, Gulf Oil, Chrysler and ITT became sizeable investors in downtown realty in the 1960 decade. A number of leading investment banking firms now have real estate departments majoring in downtown property for their own and client accounts.

While the urban postwar metropolitan realty boom may have peaked out in 1970 due to high money rates, possible overbuilding in certain areas, cut-backs in space (especially by brokerage firms), some tenant militancy, and scaling down of corporate urban office space requirements due to the recession, we see no dangerous clouds in the long-term horizons for well-run companies specializing in modern, centrally located urban realty.

CHAPTER VI

Real Estate Equity Trusts

THE modern real estate equity trust (REIT) dates from the Real Estate Investment Trust Act, which became effective January 1, 1961. No great attention was paid to this act or to its provisions until 1969. Prior to that year there was outstanding no more than $500 million in market value of all REIT transferable certificates. In 1969, however, this updated realty security caught on. New capital issues of REITs totaled over $1 billion in 1969, and over $1.2 billion in 1970.

What caused this upsurge in popularity? This type of investment trust is actually a counterpart of the mutual investment fund. It enables the small investor to participate in large scale realty projects, and to benefit from continuous professional supervision of his investment. REITs gathers the sums required to finance, in part, the vast home and building developments planned or in progress. The REIT affords to the investor the advantages of marketable liquidity and a portfolio diversified over many properties.

Further elements in the popularity of REITs is the tax shelter it provides, somewhat similar to municipal bonds; and the traditional usefulness of real estate holdings as an effective hedge against inflation.

Distinguishing Features

To qualify for its special status a REIT must be organized and operated under the following provisions:

1. The REIT cannot be a corporation, but must be an association or trust, managed by trustees, with transferable certificates of beneficial interest held by more than 100 people. No five of such investors may own or control in total more than 50 percent of a trust's shares.
2. The trust must have 75 percent or more of its assets in real estate, mortgages, cash or equivalents.
3. The trust must generate 75 percent of its income from real estate holdings, mainly rents and mortgage interest. In addition, the gross income from real estate rent, dividends, interest, or capital gains on sale of securities must equal at least 90 percent of all income. (No in and out realty speculators need apply!)
4. Assuming the foregoing provisions are met, the trust, to qualify for tax exemption must distribute at least 90 percent of all ordinary income to its shareholders each year. Such distributions are taxable to the individual as ordinary income, at his own tax bracket rate.

The trust itself pays no tax on income thus distributed, and avoids the dual taxation inherent in most corporate cash dividend payments. A trust has two options on realized capital gains: it can retain these for reinvestment, or declare them and pay capital gains taxes thereon.

Investment Procedures

Equity trusts concentrate primarily on long-term ownership of real property which may (or may not) be subject to mortgages or other liens. The investment may be in raw land (customarily leased out to produce income), or in improved income-producing realty such as residential, commercial, or industrial properties. The defense against inflation provided by realty ownership is well documented. Favorably located income-producing property has enhanced steadily in market value in every decade of this century. Current rental receipts may not accurately reflect the long-term earning power of any given property. While the book value of the property may remain unchanged, actual market value of the equity may increase significantly in an inflationary economy.

Depreciation

The basic source of tax shelter in a REIT is found in the relatively liberal allowance for depreciation, allowed by IRS for real estate. Most newly acquired buildings are depreciated on the 125 percent declining balance method, which concentrates most of the depreciation within the first 10 years. At the end of that period, when most of the allowable depreciation on the property has been taken, the trust may sell it, with the difference between depreciated book value and the selling price reported as a capital gain, and taxable at the proper rate for such.

Cash Flow and Taxation

Accordingly a different type of security analysis is required for a REIT than for the common stock of corporations. What is really important in a REIT is the cash flow, and not the traditional "net after taxes!" for most of these equity trusts dividends represent a distribution of cash flow. Of this, only that part of the dividend which represents actual net income is taxable to shareholders. To illustrate: First Union, a sizeable trust owning modern office buildings in many cities, paid 84 cents a share in 1969. Of this, 52 cents a share was reported as return of capital (depreciation) and 32 cents in taxable income. For an investor in the 50 percent bracket, this was equivalent to a $1.36 dividend on a representative common stock.

Investment Media

Actually, a REIT can be divided into two categories: Equity Trusts and Mortgage Trusts, depending on the type of investment in which most of its funds are placed. A number of the larger trusts underwritten in 1969/70 combined these investment media. (We will take up Mortgage Trusts in the next chapter).

Equity Trusts specialize in the long-term ownership of real property, with rents as their major source of income. Property selected for purchase may be residential, commercial or industrial, or even vacant land. Income producing structures generate excess depreciation, which can be distributed to shareholders largely tax free. Land, however, throws off no depreciation, and rentals from it are classified as ordinary income, taxable when distributed to holders.

Some of the more aggressive trusts stress capital gains and are eager to sell a property whenever the price offered for it is substantially above its cost (and well above depreciated book value).

Management

A REIT, to be successful, must have a competent management team experienced in appraisal, operation, financing, purchase, sale, and leasebacks of real estate. Many of the leading trusts are affiliated with large banks, insurance or mortgage companies which already have seasoned staffs of skilled and sophisticated reality managers. While it may seem quite easy in boom times for a team of businessmen to buy an office building, run it for a few years and sell it at a profit, during a recession, specialized experience and expertise are required. Real estate values are based on location and long-term utility. Tax factors and desirable (and safe) degrees of leverage are far more important in this field than in standard manufacturing or service companies. Amateurs may handle these things satisfactorily on a short-term basis, but it takes professionals with judgment, vision, and contacts to operate and finance realty and to avoid costly errors over the long run.

REIT investment decisions are customarily made by a board of trustees. Quite generally trusts employ, in addition, management companies to handle routine operations of properties, and to provide periodic reviews of investment holdings.

Income on REIT equity shares may provide returns of from 6 to 10 percent, depending on available income and market factors affecting share prices. Capitalizations of many trusts include debt securities as well as trust shares, and quite frequently warrants as well. Since trusts consistently pay out almost all the income they receive, there is little plow-back (except perhaps in retentions of capital gains from properties sold).

Trusts with programs for long-range expansion will thus plan to do additional financing with some frequency. The ideal way to do this is to sell common stock at times when it can be marketed at a substantial premium over its book value; and to sell debentures when interest rates are favorable. Under such conditions the new money benefits present shareholders by: 1. creating additional leverage with debt securities, 2. expanding the annual flow of distributable income, and 3. stock exchanged for realty which may acquire properties yielding 9 percent to 12 percent, with stock paying perhaps only 5 percent to 8 percent.

A REIT in fact may have an advantage in acquiring prime real estate because it can buy for cash, in a tax free exchange of stock, or with tax deferred debentures. It can also finance joint ventures with responsible developers.

Over the years, a well run REIT should be able to increase its payout to shareholders and at the same time enhance its asset values. As leases expire, renewals are generally at higher rates, and the larger income resulting is swiftly reflected in higher market values for the properties owned. Finally, a REIT may shelter hidden assets in its balance sheet, because depreciated book values are commonly substantially below "going" market values.

A REIT may thus achieve investment results not produced by the general run of stock equities, with a consistent rise in yield to holders, accompanied by built-in enhancement of the total market of the trust equity.

Because of the urgent demand for new construction and the almost chronic shortage of mortgage money, there is a genuine economic need for REITs as substantial and available reservoirs of realty capital funds.

PREIT

A good example of the equity trust is Pennsylvania Real Estate Investment Trust. It has been in operation for nine years and has had an excellent record. For the final year ended August 31, 1970, net earnings were 96 cents a share on the 1,154,489 shares outstanding, up 15 percent over 1969. Dividends were 80 cents for each year.

Again at August 31, 1970, PREIT showed a total investment in real estate of $65 million representing full or partial ownership of 13 shopping centers in eight states, 9 apartment houses, 6 industrial buildings, a Philadelphia office building, a high-rise motor hotel in New Orleans, and 50 undeveloped acres in a favorably located Pennsylvania area. These are modern properties with high occupancy rates and overall vacancies of less than one percent.

Here is a trust in active operation long enough to establish its earning power and growth potentials. In 1970 the stock became listed on AMEX and increased its dividend to 85 cents, compared with an 80 cent rate over the preceding 3 years.

Other issues on any sophisticated shopping list would include among equity trusts:

American Realty Trust
Citizens & Southern Realty Investments
Clevetrust Realty Investors
Equitable Life Mortgage & Realty
First Memphis Realty
First Union Realty Trust
Greenfield Real Estate Investment Trust
Hubbard Real Estate Investments
Kavanau Real Estate Trust
Mass. Mutual Mortgage & Realty Investments
National Realty Investors
Real Estate Investment Trust of America
Saul Real Estate Investment Trust
U.S. Realty Investment
Wachovia Realty Investment

There are in addition a number of newer trusts (like some of those listed) that start out dedicated to both mortgage and equity investments in their portfolio.

In any event we have here an exciting new investment sector wherein the shares pay dividends for higher than common stocks in general and their bonds pay from 7¾ to around 8¼ percent depending on their investment quality. Income-minded investors definitely should look to REITs to solve at least in part the problem of rewarding long-term investment in marketable realty securities.

CHAPTER VII

Mortgage Trusts

MORTGAGES are generally of two classes—long-term and construction. The long-term variety has historically been acquired and held principally by savings banks, building and loan associations, pension and endowment funds, and insurance companies. Construction loans have customarily been provided by commercial banks, savings and loans, and finance companies. Within the past three years, however, a relative newcomer in construction loans has entered the picture in a big way. It's the mortgage trust—actually a REIT that invests primarily in realty mortgages, rather than equity ownerships.

The mortgage trust is structured for tax shelter in the same way as the equity trust (REIT): 1. no Federal income tax is assessed so long as 90 percent or more of net income is paid to shareholders, 2. investments are predominantly in real estate, 3. 90 percent or more of net income (after expenses of operating the trust have been deducted) is "passed through" to shareholders (quite like a mutual fund), and 4. operating expenses consist of fees to advisors, interest on money borrowed to finance portfolio investments, and reserves for loan losses.

Mortgage Portfolios

Mortgage trusts in general concentrate on building or construction loans because these pay the highest interest returns.

Nongovernment construction lending in 1970 was in the order of $60 billion, with mortgage trusts providing in excess of $2½ billion. Three years earlier the MT participation in this loan sector was only about $250 million—so you can see how fast the MT's are growing. The MT is really just a new way of conducting a very old business.

The procedures of construction financing for builders and developers are roughly as follows:

Before a sizeable building project gets underway, a permanent lender, often an insurance company, is lined up to make a firm commitment for a long-term mortgage on the property after construction has been completed and proper evidence of this completion (usually a certificate of occupancy) has been presented. (Occasionally a construction loan may be made by an insurance company to an especially strong or well-qualified builder, but the inducement would be an extra high interest rate or an equity "kicker.") Fortified by this long-term loan commitment, the MT is ready to proceed. It secures a first mortgage, so that if anything goes wrong it can foreclose.

Loan valuations are fairly standard, with most MT's limiting the principal amount of the loan to 75 percent of the estimated value of the completed (or improved) property. If the builder quits on the job, or operates in an unsatisfactory manner (failure to follow specifications, inferior or shoddy construction, delay, nonpayment to suppliers, etc.), there is a clause in the loan agreement whereby the MT can terminate the loan, and get another builder or contractor to complete the project.

In the money market of 1970, construction loans provided yields as high as 15 percent to 18 percent. It was probably these high yields that attracted new money so magnetically into MT's, and a spate of major underwritings of new mortgage trusts. The prospects for continued high interest rates on construction loans for some years ahead appear favorable, so that shares in selected MT's should prove rewarding and gain in popularity among investors.

Management Criteria

It is obvious that in 1970, with interim building loans in such great demand and rates so attractive, MT's should prosper. In the long run, however, quality of management is bound to "separate the sheep from the goats"; for there are many pitfalls in this business. It takes experienced realty bankers to appraise construction loans, evaluate reliability and capability of builders; and aggressively follow-up and evaluate a contractor's performance and capability all along the way.

A successful MT must be able to anticipate a bad loan situation and have the ability to handle it if it occurs. Because of the expertise, vigilance, and practical experience required, MT's affiliated with some of the big banks and insurance companies with a built-in top flight realty advising group are going to prove more successful than smaller trusts with less talented or resourceful managements.

Financial Acumen

In addition to managerial vigilance in skillfully shepherding the construction of an edifice from excavation to occupancy, financial acumen is required. It is essential to: 1. gather the needed capital funds, usually by an original public offering of mortgage trust plain debentures, convertibles, shares and warrants (or combinations of these) and 2. expand capital funds prudently by short-term borrowing and by selling additional equity (or convertible debentures) from time to time, when they can be sold at prices representing premiums over book value.

MT's (and REITs), because they cannot retain large

chunks of income but must pay most of it out, have to go to the security markets with some frequency, if they expect to grow. They are somewhat like public utilities in that they are quite limited in the amount of income in each year they can retain and plow-back.

While the projection of earnings for 12 to 18 months ahead can be quite accurate in the case of an MT, longer-range forecasting is more difficult. As long as MT's maintain a good "spread" between the cost of money and the interest yield they will do well. This may not be so easy to do in future years, if interest rates fall and it becomes difficult to keep fully invested in quality loans.

The many new mortgage trusts that emerged in 1969 and 1970 and their huge total reservoir of lendable funds suggest that there may arise increasing competition for the choicest loans. This competition may: 1. drive down interest rates, and 2. cause some MT's to accept poorer quality (riskier) loans. If an MT incurs losses and write-offs on bad loans, earnings will suffer and it may be difficult to sell additional shares at above book value—which is the name of the game.

In assuring origination and a steady flow of high quality loans and professional capability in averting or fielding sour loans effectively those MT's affiliated with major financial institutions will probably be the long-term winners. Because construction loans mature from 12 to 18 months, a steady supply of new ones to replace the maturing ones is essential. If the MT has as an affiliate a mortgage or commercial bank, life insurance company, or a realty development company, it has a virtually "captive" source of new loans coming its way. The MT can also call upon the financial adroitness of its sponsoring affiliate for shrewd liability management and timely equity financing.

Finally, as long as income flows remain high, portfolio losses negligible, and income from fees steady and rising, MT's will look good and satisfy their shareholders. Because, however, we have such a short history of earnings of MT's, and few have been around long enough to document the quality (or its lack) of their managements, we may have to wait a bit before the General Motors or the IBM of this industry emerges.

Investment Criteria

In the selection of MT shares, the investor should give careful consideration to: 1. management and affiliation, 2. the indicated yield on the shares (it should be well above prevailing rates offered savings institutions), 3. the character and diversification of loans in the MT portfolio, 4. the ratio of market price to book value (the best MT may sell at 1½ times book, depending on market conditions, but you should strive to buy a good issue at or below book), 5. the Price/ Earnings ratio (in mid-1970 this averaged about 10½ times), 6. the leverage afforded (look for something around 3 to 1, debt versus equity), and 7. the annual growth rates in earnings and book value.

There is a strong trend away from specialization in these realty trusts, and "third generation" trusts, sponsored by major financial institutions are designed for large scale investment in equities and mortgages—either or both. Illustrative of this trend are Connecticut General Mortgage and Realty Investment, Wachovia Realty Investments, and Chase Manhattan Mortgage and Realty Trust, all launched in 1970.

For further guidance in the evaluation of MT's, the general structure of one as set forth in its offering prospectus might be useful. Under date of October 1, 1970, BT Mortgage Investors offered $10 million in 6¾ percent convertible subordinated debentures due October 1, 1990, together with 600,000 shares of beneficial interest in units consisting of 6 shares and $100 in debentures at $250. Figuring the bonds at par, the indicated price per share was $25.00. Further, the debentures are convertible into shares @ $26.25.

The offering circular recites that "substantially all the net proceeds from this offering will be converted in existing mortgages, pursuant to agreements with Sackman Gilliland." BT Advisors, Inc., a subsidiary of Bankers Trust New York Corp., is the advisor to the trust, and its officers are all executive officers of Sackman Gilliland Corp., owned by BTNY. This BT realty group, at July 31, 1970, supervised real estate and mortgage loan investments aggregating approximately $1.2 billion, so you can see the probable source of most BT Mortgage Investors loans.

The stated investment program includes the purchase of real estate equity participations and investments, as well as first mortgage, long- and intermediate-term loans, first mortgage construction and development loans, junior mortgage, "wrap around" mortgage loans, and gap loan commitments for a fee. The prospectus lists the immediate investments planned, which are mainly in apartment house mortgages—construction, intermediate, and permanent.

At the conclusion of the financing, 608,000 shares of beneficial interest were outstanding, and there was $10 million in debentures. The trust also anticipates making substantial use of borrowed capital—bank loans, commercial paper, long-term, and convertible debt.

The prospectus spells out as well the details of operation, income distribution, and tax shelter.

As a variation from combining debt with equity, First of Denver Mortgage Investors offered under prospectus dated October 6, 1970, units @ $20.00 each, consisting of one share of beneficial interest and a warrant to buy another share at $20.00, through October 6, 1975. This financing provides for ultimate doubling of paid in equity capital, as and when warrant holders exercise their rights.

The mortgage trust industry apparently has a bright future.

It would be our hope that its expansion is achieved through the growth of the substantial institutions now in existence, rather than by proliferation of a spate of new and less resourceful MT's, which through poor origination, capability, inadequate loan supervision, and amateur liability management, may make unpleasant financial waves; and by their poor operating results and market performance tend to disenchant investors as to the romance and potentials of this attractive industry. MT's will have constant future needs for ready access to the money and securities markets, and their financing will be more satisfactorily arranged in a confident industrial climate.

City Investing Mortgage Group

City Investing Mortgage Group, as its name indicates, specializes in mortgages rather than equity ownership. It has been doing an excellent job. For its first fiscal year, ended October 31, 1970, audited figures revealed loans and commitments of $157.6 million, about 53 percent in construction and development loans (customarily maturing within 18 months and commanding interest rates substantially higher than those prevailing for permanent mortgages). Of these loans, about $80 million were in mortgages on office buildings and garden apartments. Net earnings were $1.28 per share on the 3,405,000 shares outstanding, with $1.26 paid out in dividends for the year.

As a new trust, the earnings build-up was slow, but increased as its funds were invested. Per share net which was only 23 cents in the first quarter rose to 40 cents in the last quarter of the fiscal year. For fiscal 1971, our guess would be a net in the order of $1.90 and a payout of at least $1.75, generating excellent dividend return on the stock trading as this was written at 17¾.

CIMG illustrates well the benefits a mortgage trust can

gain by association with a large scale real estate compan (City Investing Company), because it was able in fiscal 197 to originate almost half of its loans and commitments.

Other mortgage trusts would include:

Associated Mortgage Investors
BT Mortgage Investors
Chase Mortgage Trust
Connecticut General Mortgage and Realty
Continental Mortgage Investors
Fidelity Mortgage Investors
First of Denver Mortgage Investors
Galbreath First Mortgage Investments
Larwin Mortgage Investors
Lomas & Nettleton Mortgage Investors
Medical Mortgage Investors
MONY Mortgage Investors
Republic Mortgage Investors
Sutro Mortgage Investment Trust

CHAPTER VIII

Federal National Mortgage Association
"Fanny Mae"

ON Monday, August 31, 1970, a new symbol appeared on the stock ticker, FNM. On that date the 8.5 million shares of common stock of Federal National Mortgage Association were admitted to trading on NYSE. The issue immediately became an active one, with 547,000 shares changing hands during the first week (ended September 4, 1970), and prices rising from 46¾, the opening sale, to 51⅜.

Fanny Mae, quite unknown to the rank and file of investors when it traded over-the-counter prior to listing, is an impressive company. It ranks as the 13th largest American Corporation, with assets of approximately $14 billion, mostly invested in real estate mortgages. Its earnings have been volatile, for reasons we shall outline, but its future is interesting, if not exciting. FNM is the standout corporation in the real estate industry, with a stature comparable in its field to IBM in computers and General Motors in automobiles.

History

Fanny Mae was not always as big and impressive. It started out in 1938 as a minor government agency, designed to function as a central mortgage bank. As such, it was run on an allotment of funds in the Federal budget; and these funds were not provided in sufficient amounts either to finance large scale purchases of mortgages or to assure liquidity in the mortgage market during periods of credit stringency.

In 1968, Fanny Mae was redesigned as a full-scale central mortgage bank, implementing the Housing Act of 1968. Under that legislation, within a five-year period Fanny Mae was to become a publicly-owned company with its shares broadly held by companies and individuals active in housing and home finance, and customers (buying or sellers of mortgages) of Fanny Mae.

In April, 1970, public stockholders elected 10 men of a 15 man Board of Directors, with President Nixon appointing the minority five. Continuing as President was Allen O. Hunter, sometime Congressman from California, who succeeded Raymond H. Lapin in the presidency in November, 1969.

Mr. Lapin had held the view that profits of Fanny Mae were secondary to the obligation of the company to sustain the home mortgage market; and in 1968–69 Fanny Mae purchased about $5 billion in FHA and VA guaranteed mortgages to support the housing industry. As a result, heavy short-term borrowing was done at progressively higher interest rates, and in January, 1970, cost of (then) current borrowings was about 8.70 percent, while the average yield on the mortgage portfolio was about 7.90 percent.

By March of 1969, however, this negative yield had been corrected, with the mortgage return advancing to 8.09 percent and borrowing costs down to 7.89 percent. The interest differential in the Company's favor continued to increase. Earnings for the second quarter were 24 cents a share, and have improved since then. It has been calculated that if the total weighted cost of interest on Fanny Mae's $12 billion of debt (as of July 15, 1970), declined by one percent, the savings in a full year would equal $7.50 a share of FNM common.

New Status

As a government sponsored, publicly-traded and privately-held company, Fanny Mae offers in its common stock a unique security to investors. Everyone who favors real-estate-oriented equities accents the leverage factor. FNM is no doubt the most highly leveraged blue chip on NYSE. As of March 31, 1970, stockholders' equity stood on the books at $294 million, and total debt at $12,227,000,000. This remarkable ratio will probably be modified in due course as more common stock is sold to the public. Much enthusiasm for FNM, however, obviously centers around this high leverage whereby rate reductions in interest paid, high average returns on mortgage portfolios, economies in operation, and increases in fees may be swiftly and even dramatically translated into net per share. This leverage can also work in reverse, of course, as was illustrated in the last quarter of 1969.

Operations

Since September 30, 1969, when government ownership ceased and preferred stock previously owned by the U. S. Treasury was retired, operations of Fanny Mae have greatly expanded. The essential and original function of the corporation is to provide continuous liquidity in the mortgage market by buying and selling (historically far less frequently) Federal-backed mortgages.

In the 1969–70 period, money available for investment in mortgages was in short supply and those institutions customarily supplying funds to home and apartment builders and owners (savings bank and S & L associations), had to sell home mortgages out of their portfolios to Fanny Mae, to generate the funds they needed to create new mortgage loans. (Had these thrift institutions been unable to raise cash in this manner, the mortgage market would have been in virtual chaos).

Theoretically, when the mortgage market becomes easier (in 1970, the bank prime interest rate was lowered from 8½ percent in March to 6¾ percent at the year's end) Fanny Mae will sell back packets of these mortgages to the savings banks and S & L's. Meanwhile, the policy of Fanny Mae is to reduce its buying as institutional needs for funds decrease.

The actual buying is done at weekly auctions in which typically, Fanny Mae might buy, or more accurately, "commit to buy," a total of say $150 million in FHA and VA mortgages. FNM charges the seller a fee which may range between ½ and 1½ percent, depending on the length of the commitment period, usually 90 days or 180 days. The sellers pay these fees for the right to sell mortgages up to a specified amount. For example, a savings bank might agree to sell to Fanny Mae up to $10 million in mortgages at an agreed price, say 97 in 90 days. It might wind up actually selling only $5 million, but would still pay the "standby" fee on the $10 million.

Income Sources

The principal and underlying source of income for Fanny Mae is the interest it collects on its portfolio of Federally guaranteed home mortgages. This portfolio, at July 30, 1970, was approximately $13.7 billion, with an average yield of about 8½ percent. This yield is quite dependable because, while there is a "roll over" of maturing mortgages each year, the bulk of liens held are long-term.

A second source of Fanny Mae's income are the commitment fees outlined above. These fees expand when money is tight, and tend to decline when the lending institutions have adequate funds to create mortgages. A third source of revenue is in possible capital gains on mortgages sold.

Fanny Mae has exerted a pervasive and constructive influence in the home mortgage industry. It stimulated new housing starts in a year (1969) when conventional housing starts were "off" more than 30 percent. It has encouraged pension funds to buy government guaranteed mortgages; and sponsored the legislation that created a secondary market for conventional mortgages. It has a construction loan program for moderate income housing, finances nonprofit hospitals, and cooperates with Government National Mortgage Association in loans for low-income housing.

Fanny Mae has also upgraded the efficiency of its operation and reduced by 40 percent the former civil service staff that operated the association. In August, 1970, Fanny Mae reduced the fees it pays to mortgage bankers and other agencies that service the mortgages in its portfolio from ½ percent to ⅜ percent. This reduction may save Fanny Mae over $2 million annually.

Financing

To be able to buy mortgages in volume and to finance its portfolio holdings, Fanny Mae is a huge borrower. It has borrowed traditionally by discount notes running variously from 30 to 270 days, and by debentures. In 1969–70, it faced a rather serious problem. Most of the debt incurred and outstanding was short-term. At July 1, 1970, total debt was about $13 billion and the average maturity about one year and five months. Obviously, this was a lopsided maturity structure and needed correction. Lengthening of maturities by selling longer-term debentures, when the market may permit is a long-term corporate objective. This policy aims to reduce the dependency on the short-term money markets and to stabilize and enhance earning power by widening the percentage spread between interest earned and interest paid. Four major Wall Street firms most sophisticated in money markets, who are the financial shepherds of FNM, will be giving this restructuring their continuous attention. In addition to the stretch-out in debenture maturities, more equity money will be raised.

On this point, it was announced on September 23, 1970, that rights would be offered to FNM stockholders to purchase one new share for each 8 shares held. (As of August 3, 1970, there were 8,538,604 shares outstanding). The "rights" offering should bring in more than $50 million in new equity money, and significantly expand the company's credit base.

Conclusions

Fanny Mae plays an indispensible part in home mortgaging; and its dual function of stabilizing the market and assuring a dependable supply of mortgage funds at all times, together with government sponsorship, assure this huge institution a permanent place in our financial spectrum.

Further, the stock is held in large amounts by leading companies in banking, building and construction, who will see to it that the FNMA Board of Directors includes able and experienced men in the mortgage banking field.

FNMA, formerly one of the least known and least understood among the major companies listed on NYSE, now is an actively traded issue with strong market sponsorship. The present dividend of 96 cents will probably be increased, if the earnings predicted by many responsible financial analysts materialize.

For 1969, reported net earnings per share were $2.50 (adjusted for the 4 for 1 split, but not for the new rights offering). Expectations for 1970 are around $1.25. However, the massive portfolio of mortgages providing a stabilized high interest return, matched with declining interest rates on borrowed money, provides the basis for expectation of rapid gains in earnings at FNMA. A per share net of possibly $5.25

seems reasonably predictable for 1971, and some portfolio managers are talking about $7.00 for 1972.

If these predictions are valid, it would appear the FNMA common selling as this was written at 53, could move to a much higher price level. Rising earnings in fashionable stocks are usually reflected both in higher market prices and enhanced price/earnings multiples. A multiple of 20 for FNM would not seem excessive. In any event, it would be inconceivable to write a book on marketable realty investments and not have a chapter on the most eminent one—Fanny Mae.

CHAPTER IX

Land Values in Lumber, Paper, and Plywood Companies

AMONG the major assets of nearly all lumber, paper, and plywood companies are their significant holdings of timberlands. These were acquired quite logically as these companies expanded, to assure supplies of basic raw materials needed for operations in current and future years. It would be silly to put up a $20 million pulp and paper plant without having at hand a dependable and plentiful source of low-cost timber. Nearness is important to minimize transportation costs. Many mills are in fact, located in the middle or at the edge of large forest tracts.

Thirty years ago nobody paid much attention to these holdings because land and lumber were plentiful and cheap, and many of these forest lands were acquired at only a few dollars an acre. There was neither a scarcity of lumber nor of land. Now, however, with the forests of Europe heavily depleted, North American timber is becoming increasingly valuable, and the demands of a rising population for living space are, each year, extending the sprawl of industrial, residential, and vacation communities deeper and into vacant and wooded lands. Thus, it is that extensive acreages owned by wood-oriented industrial companies are now important items on their balance sheets, and influential in determining the worth and potentials of their common stocks.

The location and accessibility of land, the kinds and quality of trees growing on it—hardwood or softwood, such as Southern Pine, or Douglas Fir in the Northwest,—are factors to be considered in the elevation of these timber holdings. Several companies list in their annual reports the values at which assets are carried; and these evaluations are almost always understated, that is, below prevailing market prices.

To outline the overall importance of these land holdings for the benefit of investors seeking real property values in the stocks they buy, we are tabulating on the next few pages the woodland holdings (in 1970) of a group of quite well known companies; and in the Appendix you will find useful stock data about each of them—number of shares outstanding, trading symbols, and high-low price range in 1970.

These companies are all of substantial stature, and their shares are held by hundreds of institutional investors.

Company Acreage Holdings

Arcata National owns 10,800 acres of redwood timberland in Northern California. Additional land, however, taken over by the government was valued in August, 1970, at $121,-585,000; and this appraisal was to be used in negotiations with the government for exchange of government timberlands and cash in settlement of Arcata's claim.

Boise Cascade owns 1,728,000 acres and controls 4,584,-000 acres of timberlands in Idaho, Oregon, Washington, California, Minnesota and North Carolina; Ontario and New Brunswick in Canada; and in the Philippines and Colombia, South America. In 1970, 200,000 additional timber acres were acquired in Louisiana and Texas. The company also has a joint interest in 443,000 acres, in Louisiana and Texas. This was all carried on the books at $77.3 million net value; and represented estimated reserves of 11 billion board feet of saw timber and 44.7 million cords of pulpwood.

Crown Zellerbach owns or controls about 3 million acres

of timberland in Oregon and Washington, principally pulp-wood, with approximately 20 percent to 25 percent Douglas Fir, suitable for lumber or plywood; 841,000 acres in Louisi-ana and Minnesota of pine and hardwood; 140,000 addi-tional acres in California, Oregon and Washington, and 1.2 million acres in British Columbia. Estimated reserves were placed at 8 million cords of pulpwood and 10½ billion board feet of saw timber. Net value—$38.1 million.

Diamond Shamrock at December 31, 1969, held leases on about 1,260,000 net acres (excluding Colombia, South America), of which 420,000 were considered proven for oil and gas production.

A very large landholder is Georgia Pacific, which owns 4.5 million acres of timberland (3.5 million in the United States), comprising Douglas Fir, California redwood, pine, spruce and other hardwood and softwood varieties. In addition, GP holds rights on 1.5 million acres containing 209 natural gas wells and 234 million tons in bituminous coal reserves. These were given a $266 million net value.

Great Northern Nekoosa controls 2,700,000 woodland acres in Maine (2,252,000 owned and 448,000 leased); and also has 189,000 timberland acres owned or leased in Geor-gia. The timber is principally suited for pulpwood and ap-praised by the company at a net value of $17.6 million.

Hammermill Paper owns 162,000 timber acres in Pennsyl-vania and controls an additional 150,000 acres in Alabama, mainly suitable for pulpwood, with a net value of $7.3 mil-lion.

International Paper is a real giant in land owning. In the U.S. it owns 6,519,000 acres and leases 362,000. In Canada, I.P. owns 1,357,000 acres and leases 15,128,000. The grand total is 23,366,000 acres, mainly for lumber, plywood and pulp. Also, I.P. has mineral rights to 5 million acres. Net valua-tion given was $153.8 million.

Kimberly Clark Co. has $36.8 million in net value of timber, of which 1.3 million acres in the U. S. are owned; and the rest is in cutting rights.

Marcor, Inc., which owns Container Corp., owns or has cutting rights on 779,000 acres mainly in Georgia and Florida, and has a 49 percent interest in 194,000 acres additionally. These holdings are given a net value of $51.8 million.

Masonite has acquired 470,000 acres of hardwood in Mississippi, California, and Pennsylvania, and has mineral rights on another 170,000 acres.

Mead Corp. owns 387,000 acres and controls 289,000 additional acres. A 50 percent owned affiliate owns 1,422,000 acres of timberland and has rights to 200,000 more. These stands are located throughout the U. S. and Canada, and are principally utilized for pulpwood. Other affiliates own 60,000 acres in British Columbia. Land net value is stated at $38.5 million.

Potlatch is a solid land owner, with 595,000 acres in Idaho and Washington, 531,000 in Arkansas; and 240,000 acres in Minnesota, principally for saw timber and pulp. The total 1,366,000 acres is given a net value of $43.2 million.

St. Regis Paper is one of the majors and assures its supply of lumber, plywood, and pulp far into the future by ownership of 2,700,000 acres and control of 5,500,000 additional located in the South, Northeast, Northwest and Canada. These assets are given a net value of $70.7 million.

Scott Paper owns, manages, or leases 3 million acres of timberland in Washington, Alabama, Mississippi, Maine, British Columbia, and Eastern Canada, providing the raw material for pulpwood for paper production. Net value is placed at $57.9 million. Also, a 50 percent owned company has 460,000 Canadian acres.

Union Camp owns or controls 1,670,000 acres of timberland for lumber, pulpwood, and plywood in Alabama, North and South Carolina, Georgia, Virginia, and Florida. Mineral exploration rights have been granted on over 500,000 acres. Net land valuation is $32.8 million.

U. S. Plywood-Champion owns 1,687,000 acres and has rights to 1,313,000 additional acres of timberland in North America. Net land value is slated at $144 million. Company lands in Western U. S. and Alaska contain lumber reserves (Douglas Fir, hardwood and pine), estimated at 13¾ trillion board feet.

Westvaco Corp. owns 1.2 million acres of Southern timberlands for pulpwood and paper, with net value of $19.2 million. Other corporate realty includes housing projects and an industrial park.

Weyerhaeuser Co. is the largest lumber products company in the world, and has an immense asset in the 5.6 million acres of timber it owns in Alabama, Arkansas, California, Mississippi, North Carolina, Oklahoma, Oregon, and Washington. In addition, it has cutting rights on 9.7 million acres of woodland, world wide. Net timberland values are slated at $395.9 million.

While the foregoing catalog of land holdings may make tedious reading, it would be unthinkable to prepare a book on marketable realty securities that did not include all these wood product companies. This list is by no means complete—it just cited most of the major land owners. However, the group selected has combined raw timber holdings given a total value of over $1.6 billion, and this figure may reasonably be presumed to represent a significant understatement.

Land values are rising almost everywhere in North America, and the value of timber seems certain to be enhanced in an inflationary economy, requiring vast outlays for building and construction, and for expanding markets in plywood and paper products of all kinds—from cups, cartons and containers to throwaway dresses and surgical gowns.

Further, these companies (taking their holdings in total,

whether in acres or square miles), own more surface area than any other single industrial group. These land assets are indeed hostages-to-fortune. In the future, they should not only produce the raw wood fuel essential to mill operations for which they were acquired, but may deliver many other additional and by-product values from oil or mineral production, camp, vacation or home development, industrial parks, and increased chemical utilization of wood, bark, and sawdust.

Logging and lumber has moved out of a frontier phase to a highly automated industry. Today, there are huge machines that can cut down trees, strip them on location in the forest, and haul the processed logs swiftly to mills or to waterways for flotation downstream.

In preparing your own shopping list of rewarding realty securities, you should comb over the stock table on these companies in the Appendix, and get from a broker, advisor or an investment service, the latest earnings and trend reports on the issues that interest you. An important element in the future profitability of each is found in its timber holdings; and the nearer these are to downtown Birmingham, Atlanta, Seattle, New Orleans, Little Rock, Phoenix, Portland or Jacksonville, the more profitable they may become!

CHAPTER X

Motel and Hotel Chains

FOR centuries, inns, taverns and, later, hotels have been desirable and profitable realty holdings. Usually located on main roadways, at the centers of towns and cities, or waterside, these hostelries have occupied choice land, usually enhancing steadily in value decade by decade. In the postwar era, the traditional downtown hotel has either been supplemented or displaced by the latest jet-age hostel—the motel.

Both hotels and motels have followed the earlier pattern of the corner grocery or drugstore, and have become units in great chains. Some of these chains have, in turn, been swallowed up by still larger corporations: Sheraton by International Tel and Tel, Hilton International by Trans World Airlines, and Western International Hotels by United Air Lines.

Big hotels still have a place, however, in city centers. The Shamrock in Houston, the Americana in New York, and the Queen Elizabeth in Montreal. Modern resort hotels have flourished in such diverse holiday areas as Las Vegas, Acapulco, Hawaii, Florida, and the Caribbean Isles. But far more dynamic in recent years, however, has been the growth of motels. Great and prosperous chains have sprung up, handsomely rewarding the early investors in their publicly-held securities. Quite a few public corporations have combined the operation of both hotels and motels.

In considering any program of long-term realty investment, we are impressed by the continued attractiveness of leading motel chains: the convenient locations and modern designs of units, built-in parking lots, functional comforts, including air conditioning and T. V. sets, dining and recreational facilities (swimming pools have become almost standard equipment), electronic advance reservation systems, and reasonable costs which have stimulated motor travel and supplemented air travel, creating a great industry virtually nonexistent a generation ago.

Investment Attractions

The investment attractions of motel shares are: 1. a built-in real estate speculation, because motels are strategically located and likely to enhance in value—if only because the costs of duplication (and of material labor), are advancing inexorably with each passing year, 2. the high leverage for equity owners, because motel companies borrow more than 60 percent of total investment, 3. the rising trend in percentages of occupancies as more travelers with more money and more leisure time "hit the road," 4. expanding profits from franchising units operated by others, 5. improved profit margins, as occupancy rate moves above the "break-even" point (around 66 percent), 6. an advancing trend in daily rates, 7. inter-unit reservation referral for motorists on long trips, "locking in" customer patronage, 8. uniform design and multiple unit operation, achieving economies in construction, maintenance, accounting, central purchasing and computerization, 9. continuity of welltrained management, 10. tax shelter through favorable depreciation allowances which maximize cash flow, and 11. opportunities for capital gains as older units use up available depreciation and may be profitably sold.

The Leader

Almost every American industry produces a leader. In motels, Holiday Inns is the acknowledged leader, with total annual revenues of over $550 million. As of June 3, 1970, Holiday Inns and its subsidiaries and licensees operated 1216 inns with 168,000 rooms in the system. Of these inns, 273 were company owned and operated—the rest by licensees. For 1969, the overall occupancy rate was 73.4 percent, and average daily room revenue, $13.69. Licenses are sold for an initial fee and continuing royalties thereafter. There's a licensing agreement covering an Australian chain with 6900 rooms; and inns are in prospect in Mexico, Canada, Europe, Latin America, and Africa.

Related to inn and restaurant operation, which produced 46 percent of 1969 revenues, are: Food Service International, a subsidiary catering foods to industrial establishments, and other company divisions manufacturing furniture, equipment and carpets for hotels, restaurants and office, records, and shipping containers. Another division, TCA Industries, includes Continental Trailways (second largest American intercity bus system), which incidentally, feeds passengers to the motel chains, and Delta Steamship Lines, operating 14 American flag ocean vessels.

At July 1, 1970, debt of HIA (NYSE symbol for the Holiday Inns' common stock) stood at $254 million; there was outstanding an issue of 134,275 shares of $5 preferred stock ($100 Par), and 1,280,224 shares of Series A Special stock (convertible into 1½ shares of common); followed by 26,176,474 of common shares paying an indicated 22½ cents dividend. In mid-1970, over 100 institutional investors held approximately 2 million shares of HIA.

Marriott Corp.

Another excellent company in this general field is the Marriott Corp. grossing over $320 million. It began as Marriott Hot Shoppes, and branched out from operation of fast food restaurants and cafeterias into airline, institutional, and industrial catering services, and the operation and licensing of Marriott Inns. Marriott goes in for large motor hotels and has impressive units in Washington, Boston, Dallas, Philadelphia, Phoenix, Chicago, Houston, New York, Richmond, and Saddle Brook, New Jersey. Extensive expansion of franchised units is anticipated.

Capitalization July 1, 1970 is $125 million in long-term debt, followed by 12,425,941 shares of MHS common. A 2½ percent dividend in stock was paid to shareholders in April, 1970. Earnings have increased every year since 1959, and were 89 cents a share for fiscal 1970 (year ends July 31).

Howard Johnson

HJ got into motor lodges as a logical outgrowth of its restaurant chain, the red-roofed geographical landmarks east of the Mississippi River.

In June, 1970, HJ properties included 849 restaurants (550 owned and the rest, franchised), 25 Red Coach Grills (owned and franchised), and 410 Howard Johnson Motor Lodges (39,000 rooms), most of them franchised. By 1973, it is expected that 1000 restaurants and 450 lodges (about 25 percent owned), will be in operation.

Earnings are rounded out by a grocery products division, marketing frozen and packaged foods and ice cream through supermarkets; HoJo soft drinks; and Fast Food Service, with outlets in resort and city locations.

Total revenues are in the $300 million area. Earnings have averaged about 95 cents a share since 1964. Common stock outstanding, 10,019,177 shares, preceded by $10¼ million in long-term debt.

Travelodge International

This organization has concentrated on motels and motor hotels, usually run as joint ventures with people who actually operate them. Motels are constructed to standard specifications on leased land, and operated in accordance with the rigid standards set up by Travelodge management.

Partnership agreements cover site selection, design construction, and furnishing of each unit (frequently with financial, and mortgage placement assistance), plus continuing license fees, agreement to purchase specified items from a Travelodge supply subsidiary, and contribution to advertising and promotion programs.

This has all worked out very well and the Travelodge network at July 30, 1970, embraced 451 motels and motor hotels in 43 states, Canada, Guam, and Mexico. Motels of Australia, an associate company, operates inns on that continent, and there is also the 41 percent owned TraileRancho Corp., a trailer park company.

Of the above motels, 314 were co-owned, 109 licensed, and 28 fully owned and operated by TL.

TL stock has been quite a "swinger" in the OTC market, ranging from 1961 to 1970 between a low of 3⅛ and a high of 36¾. Earnings have been in a long-range uptrend on the common, 2,189,196 shares outstanding. Cash dividend is 25 cents.

Hilton Hotels

The major name in hotels is Hilton, which owns, leases, or manages 73 hotels and inns in big cities, led off by the Conrad Hilton, Chicago; Shamrock Hilton, Houston; the Beverly

Hilton in Los Angeles; and Hilton Hawaiian Village (all owned in fee).

Hilton Inns owns, manages, or leases inns in eleven cities, and has allotted franchises for about 30 additional inns across the country.

Earnings rose from 30 cents a share in 1964 to $2.20 in 1969, and the stock has been popular marketwise. The international hotel chain was acquired by TWA, but HLT owns 51 percent of Hilton Service, operating a reservation service for itself and TWA. There are 7,441,330 common shares of HLT preceded by $195 million in long-term debt. There is also an issue of warrants. Hilton is an excellent and representative equity in the hotel field.

Other Hotel and Motel Chains

Among other motel chains, Ramada Inns, Royal Inns, and American Motor Inns, have fine records of growth and gain, and you should also look at the Downtowner Corp. and Quality Court Motels.

In hotels, your shopping list should include Sonesta International Hotels (leading ones—the Plaza in New York and Mayflower in Washington), the Hyatt Corporation and Knapp and Loew's.

This swift resumé of hotel-motel shares should provide useful background guidance for any investments you may have in mind in this realty sector. The things to research are the: 1. quality and record of management, 2. earnings record and growth rate, 3. the capital structure, 4. return on stockholders' equity, and 5. general economic conditions.

Hostelries for travelers depend on: 1. patronage of businessmen (who are much freer spenders in prosperous times), 2. tourist and vacation travel, and 3. special room use for meetings and conventions, not to mention romance. If we continue to have high-level economic activity, well-managed inn chains may prove to be the "in" investments! But, should there occur a deep recession, then occupancies would fall below break-even levels, interest and mortgage payments would be painful to meet; and weaker companies might, in distress, sell or close down losing lodges. (There were hundreds of substantial hotels foreclosed between 1931 and 1933.)

During the good times, however, the leverage in motel shares remains highly profit-prone. Historically, capital gains of 500 percent to 1,000 percent on good motel shares within a decade have not been uncommon.

CHAPTER XI

Assorted Realty Equities

IN earlier chapters we have endeavored to assemble many quite well-known public companies, and arrange and group them into broad major categories depending on the types of realty activities in which they were principally engaged. Motels, office buildings, land developments, forest, agricultural, mineral acreage, were some of the major groups. Dozens of other companies, however, did not seem to fit neatly into any of these specific categories, so we decided to offer in this chapter comments on a random assortment of these companies, and thus provide a more panoramic realty shopping list.

McGrath Corp.

Out on the West Coast, McGrath Corp. is a major home builder-developer in the Seattle area. This company went public with 100,000 shares of common at 19½ in January, 1969. That year was a profitable one, and the company converted sales of $14.2 million into a net profit of $486,557 or $1.40 a share on the 348,075 shares outstanding. For the fiscal year ended June 30, 1970, however, sales dipped to $8.1 million and a loss of 90 cents a share (the first loss in 10 years of operation) was recorded.

This was due to extensive unemployment and drastic layoffs by the Boeing Corp. in the area. As a result, the company changed its corporate accent from building private homes to government sponsored projects, and subsidized housing, including modular, low-cost construction. The common stock (traded OTC), ranged in 1969–70 between a high of 31 and a low of three.

Arizona-Colorado Land & Cattle Co.

This Phoenix, Arizona, based company is a large owner of land in the Western States. It operates cattle ranches on over 1.3 million acres of open range and farmland; and a subsidiary runs a cattle feedlot with a capacity of 60,000 head. Other subsidiaries include a small meat packing company, a water utilization facility, a land planning and engineering firm, 92 percent of the stock of Alamosa (Colorado) National Bank, and a tungsten ore body in eastern Nevada. There are 2,674,901 common shares of AZL outstanding and listed on AMEX.

Investors Funding Corp.

This expanding corporation is essentially an urban realty company owning apartments, office buildings, shopping centers, urban building sites or leaseholds and land for development. In addition, IFC does a big mortgage business. Most realty held for investment purposes is rented for long-terms under net lease contracts whereby the lessee pays all operating expenses and financial charges—realty taxes, interest, and amortization of mortgages.

Other investments of IFC include 97 percent of the stock in Citizens Savings & Loan Co. (of Akron, Ohio), 90 percent of Citizens Bank & Trust of Wadsworth, Ohio with combined assets (December 31, 1969) of about $65 million; 31 percent of Security Title and Guaranty Co., carrying on a title insurance business in New York, New Jersey, Connecticut, and

Washington D.C.; District Realty Title Insurance Corp., Washington, D. C. (wholly-owned); Ballard Mortgage Corp.; 21 percent of Citadel Life Insurance Co. of New York; and IFC Securities Co., a securities underwriter and distributor of mutual funds.

In 1969, a quite unrelated property was acquired, P. Ballantine & Sons, for $16 million cash. This unit grossed $36.3 million in 1969, but operated in that year at a net loss.

IFC is highly leveraged, with (December 31, 1969), $181 million in long-term debt, a $257,000 minority interest, 3,733 shares of $5 preferred stock, 1,097,945 shares of Class A common ($5 par) listed on AMEX, 17,582 shares of Class B common ($5 par) and warrants to buy about 1.5 million shares of Class A with varying rates and expiration dates. Additional debt financing of $54 million was arranged during 1970. The A stock has been a volatile performer, ranging during 1969–70 between 46⅛ and 8¾.

United Artists Theater Circuit

This unique company majors in motion picture theaters, with secondary interests in shopping centers and other realty; a CATV complex comprising 14 systems in eight states; marketing of projection equipment and candy, soda, popcorn and janitor supplies, mainly to theaters; and a photographic and wide-angle projection technique. The latest UATC venture is "Minitek," an automated mini-theater for special locations (starting out with an installation near a Holiday Inn).

The big investment play, however, is in the 114 drive-in theaters and 286 traditional theaters UATC operates—230 owned in fee and 170 leased.

Revenues for the fiscal year ended August 31, 1970, were $75 million distilling into $1.33 a share on 1,617,888 common shares, trading OTC. The 1969–70 price range was between 36½ and 6¾.

U. S. Home & Development

Here's an across-the-board entry in home building. UHD (AMEX symbol for the common stock), builds and markets structures all the way from single family homes to high-rise and garden apartments, shopping centers, condominiums, and retirement homes. Further, it creates whole communities and mobile home parks. In addition, the company owns Dee Wood Industries, a lumber and household wood products units; Clearwater Concrete Industries, Inc., concrete and concrete blocks; and U. S. Home of Greenbriar, Inc., planning to create a new home community on 1300 Florida acres.

For year ended February 28, 1970, UHD had revenues of $52.5 million and earned $1.45 on its common stock (1,671,-825 shares outstanding), up from $1.02 a year earlier. The stock is an animate performer on AMEX.

Perini Corporation

Perini Corporation is a contracting and construction business that also is in real estate development, urban renewal, and operates as an owner or leaser of industrial and commercial buildings.

Real estate operations include 4005 acres near West Palm Beach, The Ajax community outside of Toronto, Ontario, three commercial and residential sites in cities near Boston, and one in Pawtucket, Rhode Island, and 700 acres and a lodge at Lake Tahoe, California.

Other nongeneral contracting investments of the Perini Corporation include a 35 percent interest in Luigi's Spaghetti Dens (a California food service chain), 10 percent of the Atlanta Braves, and 5 percent of Hamilton Petroleum, an oil drilling firm.

Sales and profits have been erratic, reflecting the ebb and

flow of contracting. Earnings for 1969 were 66 cents a share on 4,328,489 shares of PCR common listed on AMEX. There have been no dividends since 1964. In the 1960 decade annual revenues ranged between $123 and $242 million.

Tejon Ranch

This large land owner gets its revenues from oil, farming, cattle raising, and rentals.

Tejon owns a 295,000 acre ranch in Kern and Los Angeles Counties in California, plus ⅓ interest in Arvin Rock Co., a producer of sand, gravel, and aggregates. Oil production from company land has been about 800,000 barrels a year. About 14,800 head of cattle were in the 1969 year-end inventory. Earnings have been approximately 40 cents a share for the past three years on 1,248,000 shares of common trading in OTC market. Long-term debt is only $141,398.

Del E. Webb Corp.

This company could have been classified either as an owner of office buildings, a land developer, or a hotel owner. Instead of bracketing it that way, however, we are treating it as a kind of realty conglomerate.

Actually, Del E. Webb is a general contractor like the Perini Corp., and started the 1970 year with a backlog of $170,000,000. This included a $40 million job on the Kansas City Airport, a $16 million Civic Plaza and Convention Center in Phoenix, Arizona, $16 million in military housing in Hawaii, a hospital, three office buildings and two motels. In addition, Del E. Webb engages in joint ventures.

Realty owned includes the 25-story Kroger Bldg. in Cincinnati, the 20-story Traders National Bank building in Kansas City, a 17-story building in Albuquerque, New Mexico, a resort hotel, community developments in Sun City,

Phoenix, Arizona, Sun City at Tampa, Florida, and Sun City, California, plus interests in shopping centers and retirement communities.

At December 31, 1969, WBB (AMEX symbol for the common stock), had $99.1 million in long-term debt, $7.3 million in minority interests, followed by 8,045,843 common shares and 563,037 warrants to buy common at prices ranging from $6.25 (to May 1, 1975) up to $15, until October 1, 1983. No dividends have been paid, and the stock is a wide market swinger.

CHAPTER XII

Mortgage Lenders and Investors

NO consideration of marketable realty securities would be complete without coverage of the mortgage lending institutions that finance almost every substantial ownership of improved real estate. Total mortgages on real estate run into hundreds of billion dollars. They come in all sizes from a mortgage of a few thousand dollars on an individual home to a $40 million mortgage on a downtown metropolitan office building.

The leading mortgage lenders are savings banks, savings and loan associations, life and casualty insurance companies, banks and trust companies, pension and welfare funds and endowed institutions. The savings banks and savings and loan associations have traditionally majored in home mortgages, while insurance endowed institutions and welfare funds and realty trusts usually go in for bigger *ticket* mortgages on office buildings, hotels and motels, shopping centers and high-rise apartments. There are also mortgage companies that are not long-term investors but who originate and place mortgages with some of the large investors mentioned in previous chapters. For these services the mortgage companies charge fees; and generally, in addition they service the mortgages (see that interest, taxes, and insurance are paid and do the accounting) for a fee from $\frac{1}{10}$ to $\frac{1}{2}$ of one percent yearly. There are many varieties of mortgages: construction loans, long, middle, interim or short term; second or third mortgages, mortgages on property owned in fee or on leaseholds, mechanics or contractor's liens for unpaid services, and an assortment of guaranteed and insured mortgages.

Investors in marketable securities may participate in these mortgage investments through ownership in shares of commercial banks or trust companies or stock insurance companies (but realty mortgages represent only a portion of the total investment portfolios of these financial institutions); realty trusts, mortgage companies and publicly-owned savings and loan associations. Mutual savings banks, mutual insurance companies and the great majority of all savings and loan associations have no publicly-owned or market-traded capital stocks.

We have discussed the realty trusts earlier in the book. In this chapter we will outline further opportunities for equity interest in mortgages through certain savings and loan companies and specialized mortgage companies.

There are savings and loan institutions located in all fifty states, the District of Columbia, and Guam. They are variously state chartered (both stocks and mutual) under supervision of the states where domiciled; and those with Federal Charters (all mutual) subject to the supervision of the Federal Home Loan Bank Board. Across the land about 90 percent of all S&Ls are mutual but there are several hundred S&Ls with publicly-held capital stock. The majority of these are located in the state of California, where stocks are available in individual institutions as well as in holding companies representing a merger of two or more originally independent S&Ls.

Method of Operation

Savings and loan associations, whether stock or mutual, operate along almost identical lines. While the prime function of the S&L is mortgage lending, the money has to come in first. This is accomplished at the outset by paid-in capital and surplus when the S&L is founded, and steadily supplemented by money lodged in individual accounts by savers—the equivalent of deposits in a commercial or savings bank. Then, as the association grows, reserves which augment capital funds, are built up out of earnings, (and also in stock S&Ls by the occasional sale of additional capital shares). These reserves are designed to meet regulatory requirements, to provide for possible bad debts, to assure continuity of interest payments on thrift accounts.

About 75 percent of all the income of the representative S&L is derived from interest on mortgages. The most common investment is in the conventional home mortgage (one- to four-family dwellings) extending from 20 to 30 years with interest at a specific rate, and provision to amortize the mortgage through regular monthly payments till maturity. In addition, the S&L derives income from fees of one percent or two percent for arranging the mortgage; and from late payment fees, prepayment penalties, foreclosure and escrow agreement fees. Other revenues may come in from properties held as investments or from gains from property sold.

The mortgages acquired are of three main varieties: 1. "conventional" wherein the home owner sends in his checks each month and this amount is variously applied to interest, amortization, property taxes, and insurance, 2. FHA mortgages which may be on homes, multiple dwellings, office buildings and which must meet certain standards, and have their interest and principal guaranteed by Federal Housing Administration by payment of a premium of ½ percent per annum, and 3. Veterans' Administration loans guaranteed (up to 60 percent valuation) for a similar ½ percent annual premium. As of March 1, 1971, conventional mortgages carried a rate of 8 percent while FHA Loans were being made at 7 percent (plus ½ percent for the guarantee).

Savings and loan associations have traditionally offered higher interest rates to depositors than commercial or savings banks, and during the early 1960s, California associations attracted hundreds of millions of thrift dollars annually from Eastern savers because their rates were one percent or more higher than were being paid by Atlantic Seaboard thrift institutions. Not only do the savers increase the available lendable dollars but reinvestments, as loans "roll over" are often at a rate of 15 percent to 20 percent of portfolio each year. The profit of the S&L is essentially produced by the difference between interest received on mortgages, and interest paid on thrift accounts. In a highly profitable year this difference or "spread" might be as much as two percent gross. Interest on S&L accounts requires about 50 percent of annual revenues, operating expenses about 25 percent, leaving 25 percent for profit before taxes. In a stock S&L, loans may run 10 times that of book value creating a powerful leverage for the capital shares. Most S&Ls pay little or no cash dividends, plowing back earnings into higher new worth.

A typical operation of a California S&L holding company might look like this:

Year 1969

Crinoline Savings & Loan Company

Revenues	
Interest on loans	$ 8,700,000
Loan fees	2,700,000
Interest and dividends on investments	400,000
Fees and profits from rentals and land transactions	400,000
Miscellaneous	300,000
	$12,500,000
Expenses	
Interest	$ 6,000,000
General and Administrative	3,500,000
	9,500,000
Earned before federal taxes	3,000,000
Federal taxes on income	500,000
Net earnings before reserves	$ 2,500,000

There might follow an appropriation to general reserves of $2,200,000 for the year, leaving a balance of $300,000.

S&Ls are cyclical performers, making a good deal of money when housing construction and the demand for mortgage money are strong, and struggling a bit when building is slow and people have a tough time meeting mortgage payments. In the period between 1966 and 1968 in California some S&Ls had as much as 6 percent of their mortgage investments "scheduled" or in other words, they were behind in regular payments, or defaulted. The S&Ls endeavor to assist the mortgagor as much as possible, but if payments get badly in arrears the S&L may, in order to protect itself, find it necessary to foreclose and take over the property. In such cases the property may later be sold outright, or offered to another individual who will pick up, and resume payments on the "tired" mortgage.

For agile speculators trading in the right S&L stocks, particularly in the early stages of a building boom, can prove quite rewarding. Here's a swift summary of some of the more active issues at your disposal.

California Savings Loan Industry

Among all publicly-owned savings and loan associations or holding companies in the U. S., 61 percent of all assets are in California; and the three largest holding companies—Great Western Financial, First Charter Financial, and Imperial Corp. are domiciled there. These, and others we shall refer to, are powerful companies with interesting futures, but they have had some problems to contend with.

During the 1960 decade, California grew at a rate (2.4 percent annually) roughly 80 percent faster than the rest of the country. As a result, there was great demand for money for home mortgage financing. To attract this money the California associations offered passbook rates to savers, which were generally higher rates than those offered elsewhere in America; and in turn the money loaned out in mortgages commanded higher long-term rates than those prevailing in the East or Midwest. This worked out well except for one thing. The money supply was short-term (on deposit and subject to swift withdrawal by savers), while the mortgage money was tied down at specified rates for from 10 to 20 years ahead. In 1966 the interest rates elsewhere, and in 1969–70 bond interest yields available at 8 percent or more, drew off the funds on deposit at California S&Ls and made it necessary for them to borrow from Federal Home Loan Bank of San Francisco at quite high rates to meet mortgage demands and to carry scheduled (defaulted) loans. This led to earnings in 1970 which were generally lower than in 1969 and reduced market enthusiasm for S&L stocks.

Further, from 1963 to 1969 S&Ls were permitted to apply 60 percent of pre-tax income to reserves for bad debts, paying taxes only on the remainder. In 1969 however, the deductible percentage was lowered to 40 percent which increased in effect the basic tax rate from 20 percent to 30 percent, adversely affecting net earnings.

Assuming that long-term interest rates stay high, we think that California S&Ls will continue to be able to attract passbook thrift funds, and invest them at a sufficiently higher rate to produce and expand net earnings. Therefore, while S&Ls may be regarded as more volatile with respect to yearly earnings, than either banks or insurance companies, they are leveraged to generate excellent profits if the spread between passbook and lending rates is maintained.

S&Ls have developed no tradition for the payment of cash dividends, preferring to plow back profits and to reward share owners by either higher reported net worth per share or the distribution of stock dividends.

Representative S&L Companies

To offer some guidelines as to available marketable securities in this sector of the realty industry, we're supplying below capsuled vignettes of representative companies.

Great Western Financial Corp. has become the world's largest S&L holding company through merger in 1970 with LFC Financial Corporation (formerly the somewhat troubled Litton Financial). The combination joins six associations with 62 statewide offices and total assets of about $3.4 billion.

GWF (symbol for common stock on NYSE) has the problem of regenerating earning power from the LFC group but also benefits at the same time from the considerable LFC tax carry forward. For 1971, GWF might earn $1.50 a share. The 1968 high for the stock was 31.

First Charter Financial Corp. has the reputation of being the most efficiently managed of the big S&Ls with general and administrative costs averaging less than .75 percent of loan portfolio against around 1.25 percent for most others. FCT is a holding company with only one association, American Savings & Loan, which has 52 offices in the Los Angeles and San Francisco areas and about $2.8 billion in assets. The company netted $2.55 per share in 1970 and should improve to $3.00 in 1971. Issue has been paying 5 percent a year dividend in stocks.

Imperial Corporation of America is a holding company domiciled in California but with 50 percent of its $1.5 million assets in Texas, 40 percent in California and the balance in Colorado and Kansas. In total, ICA owns 14 associations with 72 offices. Stock earned 90 cents in 1970 and should increase its profits 15 percent in 1971.

Financial Federation Inc. owns eleven S&L associations in California with $1.15 billions in assets. The 3,320,000 shares of FFI listed on NYSE have been volatile in performance reflecting deficits in four out of the past five years. The outlook for 1971 and the years ahead is brighter due to heavy write-offs in 1970, and steady reduction in "scheduled" loans. The common stock is more suitable for speculators than investors, however.

Gibraltar Financial is another major S&L, with assets of over $800 million and 21 California offices as a result of their mergers with Pioneer S&L in February 1969, City S&L in July 1969, and Shasta S&L in January 1970. GFC had a consistently profitable record in the 1960 decade earning $2.25 a share in 1969. Lending volume was reduced in 1970, lowering per share net to around $1.45. We would expect an earnings' gains in 1971 and later years.

United Financial operates 14 offices in Southern California and has approximately $440 million in assets. Earnings of about 90 cents a share in 1969 and 1970 were reduced in 1970 by write-offs. Economic conditions in the area and the price of money will determine the 1971 results. Earnings of as much as one dollar a share appear possible for 1972. There are 2,826,000 shares of UFL outstanding.

Trans-World Financial owns two associations and a commercial bank in California, and a small association in Denver, Colorado. Its total assets are valued at $350 million. TWF lost 10 cents a share in 1969 and then turned around to produce a 60 cents profit in 1970. Dividends of 5 percent were paid in stock in 1968, 1969, and 1970.

California Financial operates nine offices in the San Francisco Bay area. Its assets are valued at $250 million, with 3,436,133 shares of common outstanding, earning about 50 cents a share. Westco Financial with $450 million in assets almost merged with GWF in 1970. It's rather a steady performer with an average per share net of about $1.75 from 1968 through 1970.

There are other smaller associations publicly traded, including Denver-based Midwestern Financial. Together they represent valid securities of mortgage-investing companies. There are interesting and frequently swiftly rewarding securities for nimble and perceptive market traders, but they definitely lack the dependability of earnings, dividends, and growth characteristics of good bank and insurance stocks.

Marketwise, S&L holding companies are perhaps the most erratic of financial institutions.

Mortgage Companies

Lomas and Nettleton, an aggressive Texas organization, is well on its way toward becoming the largest real estate financing company of its kind in America. As of November 1, 1970, it was servicing over $3 billion in real estate mortgages, and was manager of the relatively new L & N Mortgage Investors, a substantial provider of construction and development mortgage loans.

L & N fees are 1 percent in originating residential loans, and ¾ percent to 1½ percent on commercial loans depending on the complexity and nature of the loan. For servicing (which provides an annuity-like income) L & N charges ⅜ percent to ½ percent a year on residential loans and ⅒ percent to ¼ percent on the commercial variety.

L & N has steadily increased its net profits. They were $443,000 in 1967, $944,689 in 1968; $2,075,920 in 1969 and $2,795,589 in 1970. The stock trades OTC and has been in a rising price trend stimulated by the foregoing earnings advances. The company plans to lists its shares, in due course, on NYSE.

Mortgage Associates, Inc. is another large mortgage handler, as well as a fine moneymaker. It earned 19.3 percent on stockholders equity in 1969.

About 99 percent of Mortgage Associates' loan originations are FHA and VA backed loans. MAI has been aggressively expanding its loan originations by opening new branch offices and now has about 19 offices in seven Midwestern states. In fiscal 1970 loan originations were $127 million— 31 percent above 1969. Its service portfolio is now approximately $100 million.

Another facet for corporate earning power provides representation in insured government housing projects through the Urban Shelter Group, Inc. The first project of Urban was a joint venture consisting of 576 three- and four-room condominium-type town houses, mass produced and prefabricated.

There are about 1,150,000 common shares of MAI outstanding held by over 2,000 shareholders, and earning approximately $1.20 per share for fiscal year ended April 30, 1971.

CHAPTER XIII

Land Values in Petroleum and Mineral Companies

OF course all mineral and metal production comes from the land. Accordingly any comprehensive book on marketable realty stocks would have to include some treatment of those large and usually international companies that, by probing and prospecting and drilling, have built up huge underground stores of oil, gas, sulfur, copper, lead, zinc, nickel, gold, silver, and other widely used minerals, making possible an extensive and profitable production. The treatment of the land assets involved, however, differs from most other real estate because there is no urge to own land outright; and, to do so, considering the hundreds of millions of acres involved, would immobilize vast sums of corporate capital. Accordingly the general method employed by most companies engaged in the extraction from the ground and the treating and marketing of these valuable natural resources, is to acquire mineral rights to broad acreages with a modest down payment per acre, and to agree to pay royalties at specified rates to the actual owners of the land (without the owners performing any services, or supplying any labor or equipment in the surfacing and marketing of the subject mineral) on all commercial production. Information about lands leased, mineral rights, or the numbers and locations of acres under company control are not always found in the Annual Reports of companies, but figures are often supplied to investment services that publish annual corporation manuals.

To illustrate the extents of land areas under control of great petroleum corporations, we are listing, in the following table figures of the approximate holdings of several well-known companies:

Oil and Gas Lands Held
(in thousands of acres)

Company	North America Net Acres	Outside North America Net Acres	Total
Marathon Oil (1918)	1,508	41,700	43,208
Standard of California (1969)	26,454	105,000	131,454
Standard of Indiana (1969)	72,602	26,468	99,070
Shell Oil (1969)	15,015		15,015
Texaco (1967)	9,900	69,800	79,700
Phillips Petroleum (1969)			110,418
Gulf Oil (1969)	9,400	188,500	197,900
Getty Oil (1969)	12,441		12,441
Mobil Oil (1969)	58,500	19,000	77,500
		(Libya, Middle East, North Sea Not Stated)	
Continental Oil (1969)	26,000	215,596	241,596
Atlantic Richfield (1969)	50,900	41,200	92,100
Canadian Superior (1969)	9,198	11,367	20,565
Pacific Petroleums (1969)	8,343		8,343

It must be remembered that these figures are all at the 1969 year end, and that they may be quite different now. Also the summaries combine actual producing acreage with other acreage variously owned in fee, or on which mineral interests, leaseholds, reservations and options may apply. In general, producing acreage will be only a small portion (one percent to five percent) of total land controlled. Further, while these land spreads seem enormous, they represent in effect, remote calls on potential future oil production. Much of the acreage may never be drilled on, or may be released for want of payment of annual rental, or failure to drill on land within a specified period of time. This lease acquisition can either be done quietly for very slight rentals per acre, or it may be done by highly competitive bidding, as when the U. S. Government or a state opens acreage (on land or under water) to bids.

If a major discovery has been made in a new ar (as in Alaska in 1969) then many companies will scour the nearby terrain from both surface and air, using magnetometers; and if they like the structure they may bid eagerly for drilling rights, paying $20,000 an acre or more for the privilege. This is very "iffy" business and an oil company can lay out millions for drilling rights only to find that the rich oil structure (fanning out from the discovery well) has "gone that-a-way."

Tenneco, Inc., is a pipeline company increasingly devoted to oil production and real estate development. It has exploratory drilling interests in some 25 million acres offshore in the North Sea, Indonesia, and in Alaska and many other areas plus land it owns (Kern County Land) with an acreage larger than Rhode Island.

The big mining companies such as Newmont, Cerro Corp., Anaconda, International Nickel, ASARCO, American Metals Climax, and Homestake, are also heavily represented in mineral acreages but they do not generally report in acres under lease, but rather in terms of companies owned, proven tonnages of reserve of various mineral ores, or annual millings at certain rates of production. Thus while it is true that in buying shares in any mineral or metal company, large or small, you are purchasing either the control or use of important land areas, it is difficult to relate these assets to a specific number of acres worth a certain amount of money. The custom is rather, in mining enterprises, to value the shares, in a rule-of-thumb way, by multiplying the number of tons of ore reserves by current profit per ton realized from mining, milling, and marketing. In this mining sector while real estate holding and use is essential to corporate operations and profitability, it is very hard to convert a leasehold in the Andes or the Canadian Rockies into book value or earnings per share. Moreover, the subject craggy mining terrain is most unlikely to be upgraded, realty-wise, into a motel, a ski lodge, a shopping center, or a supermarket.

More specific relation of land to share value can be found in oil-prone land companies such as the following:

Louisiana Land & Exploration Co.

This company is primarily a large scale holder of oil and gas lands, deriving about 60 percent of its operating revenue from oil and gas royalty payments from several major oil companies; 35 percent from working interests in oil and gas wells; and the balance from bonuses, rentals, and sulphur royalties.

The land spread includes 1,527,680 acres of producing and prospective oil and gas lands, principally on- and offshore in Southern Louisiana. Of these, 594,283 acres are held in fee onshore in Louisiana, with additional holdings in 12 other States. In the Canadian Northwest, Arctic Isles, Alberta, and Manitoba. LLX (NYSE symbol for the common stock) has interests in 2,309,000 net acres. There are also land developments along the Houston Ship Canal and in Hawaii.

Net income has been steadily rising from $32 million in 1964 to over $51 million in 1970. Long-term debt is $27.8 million followed by 18,119,407 shares of common. Dividends are about 70 percent of net revenues. (Stock split 2 for 1 in 1971.)

Texas Pacific Land Trust

The trust subshares of TPL represent an unusual realty-based equity. In late 1954 the properties of the original trust were divided, with most of the land, oil, gas, and other assets, placed in TXL Oil Corp. (Acquired in full by Texaco in 1962); and TPL retaining 1,649,278 acres of surface holdings in west Texas, a perpetual sustaining royalty ($\frac{1}{128}$th) on about 85,000 producing acres, and a $\frac{1}{16}$ nonparticipating perpetual royalty interest on any minerals that may be produced from 387,000 acres of undeveloped tracts.

The royalty agreements are somewhat complicated and the largest potential for future income expansion is found in the $\frac{1}{16}$ interests on 387 acres. Net income has been running at about $1 million annually, applicable to 1,149,889 net share certificates, trading on NYSE.

CHAPTER XIV

The Summing-Up

NEVER in history has it been as easy for the average man with surplus funds to have so many options if he wishes to own real estate. He can, as he has for centuries, own land, his own house, other homes or two-family dwellings for rental and, with enough resources, larger structures and broad swaths of acreage. But for those who seek superior marketability, no details of supervision and continuous professional management, there are billions of dollars in highly marketable securities of realty or realty-oriented corporations, represented by shares, warrants and bonds. All of these are at hand for investor selection and purchase, whether he has only a few hundred dollars or a few hundred-thousand dollars available for the purpose.

Further, his selection may range from low-priced speculation in shares and warrants, to income producing corporate and realty trust equities, and high yielding bonds and attractive convertibles. The investor can, and should, get guidance for his purchases from his broker, the investment services, investment counsel, and reports direct from the trusts and corporations.

Historically, land has been man's primary source of both subsistence and wealth, and there is nothing on the horizon to suggest that land will become less desirable as a personal investment in the years to come. The rise in population, industrial activity, incomes, and standards of living assure more intensive occupancy and use of land for a myriad of purposes.

However, while land and the structures on it may be expected to advance in price over the long run with considerable predictability, the costs and incidents of ownership are going up as well.

For example, many people moved after World War II to retirement living in towns, on Eastern Long Island—from Patchogue to Montauk. They were attracted to these towns initially by the relative low cost of land and homes, and particularly by the low tax rates. Because the communities were not heavily populated and were made up mostly of older residents and summer people, these towns did not require extensive investment in fire fighting forces and equipment, police coverage or schools (because there were relatively few children of school age). In the twenty years from 1950 to 1970, however, this area about doubled in population, many industries sprang up and the whole section became exurban rather than "country." Costly new schools had to be built to educate the crop of children. More paved sidewalks, more street lights and garbage collection facilities were needed—and of course taxes went up—faster in fact, as a percentage, than the increases in property prices.

This same thing has been happening all over the country so that those who own income-producing property directly, or through stock certificates, face a steady series of rising cost for government supplied services.

In repair and maintenance the situation is no better. The costs of lumber, plywood, electrical and plumbing fixtures, paint, and the services of plumbers, carpenters, painters and landscapers are all going up. Accordingly in making realty investments, you must be assured that the managements are cost conscious, and know how to keep the margins between gross revenues and net returns attractive. In real estate, as in other security sectors, the quality and competence of management is the best assurance that an investment in realty can be both rewarding and gainful.

Another thing to always keep in mind is the change constantly taking place in realty. Today's swank area may be tomorrow's slum. Look at all of the brownstones in downtown and central Brooklyn that went from middle-class serenity to semi-ghettos within 20 years' time.

Equally, corporate investments made in foreign lands need constantly to be evaluated in relation to political and social stability. For example, not only industrial properties such as copper mines have been subject to capture in Chile, but almost as vulnerable are American-owned apartments, hotels, or office buildings.

In the Caribbean isles, the increased aggressiveness of native population, and rapid rises in local labor costs, have made retirement home and resort investment on some of these islands uncertain and possibly hazardous over the long-term.

It is now fashionable for land companies to stake out large holdings in rather undeveloped countries such as Africa, Asia, and Australia. These ventures may prove productive over a period of time, but care must be taken not to invest in another Cuba, Peru, or Chile where either insurrection or expropriation may erode or destroy the values of American-owned realty.

We do not wish to appear gloomy about the outlook for realty because indeed we are not. But we do not want you to know the risks as well as the rewards of such investments.

We are particularly impressed with the philosophy of a certain builder of high quality multiple dwelling retirement homes. These are not for sale, but for rent to oldsters. The lease, however, is only for one year, in order that rental increases may be swiftly made to offset any significant rise in operating costs or taxes.

CHAPTER XV

Charts, Tables, and Exhibits

IN this chapter we have drawn up a series of charts, tables, and exhibits that may well have cluttered the prose flow of the text had they been appended to relevant earlier chapters.

In Chapter VI we took the Real Estate Equity Trusts and outlined the various kinds of buildings customarily making up its realty portfolio. To illustrate a typical investment for a REIT, we are now assuming its equity ownership of a modern urban office building built in 1970.

This building is 37-stories high built on a choice corner plot in downtown New York City. The land—20,000 square feet was acquired at $300 a foot for a total cost of $6 million. The building, containing 400,000 square feet of rentable space, cost $16,000,000 to build and was fully rented at $10 a square foot. Because over 50 percent of the space was rented under long-term leases, to tenants with a triple A credit rating, a large insurance company took a $16,500,000 fifty year first mortgage on the property bearing interests at 8½ percent, with amortization agreed upon at 2 percent annually. (The quality of tenancy has an important bearing with an institutional lender both as to the amount and the interest of the mortgage.) With all this data at hand, we are now ready to write up a flow sheet on this venture:

Modern Office Building

Cost of Land	$ 6,000,000
Building	16,000,000
	$22,000,000
Mortgage	$16,500,000
Cash Equity Required	$ 5,500,000

Yearly Operating Statement

Annual Income	$ 4,000,000
Less Mortgage Amortization	— 320,000
Less Mortgage Interest	— 1,280,000
Less Payroll	— 300,000
Less Repair, Superintendence, Maintenance, Insurance & Real Estate	— 450,000
Less Depreciation	— 640,000
	$ 3,000,000
Income Before Taxes	$ 1,000,000
Less Income Taxed—Federal	— 415,000
State & City	— 125,000
Net After Taxes (available to the $5,500,000 equity)	$ 460,000

Obviously this return will increase as mortgage is reduced.

Depreciation is not actually paid out so that "cash flow" is really $1,100,000 a year—$640,000 plus $460,000—a 20 percent return on $5,500,000.

Representative Forest Products Companies

Company	Number of Common Shares Outstanding	Listed	Ticker Symbol	—Price Range— 1970 High	Low	Closing Price Dec. 31, 1970
Arcata National	6,317,754	NYSE	ACA	42¼	15½	20⅝
Boise Cascade	29,757,936	NYSE	BCC	75⅜	39¼	46¼
Crown Zellerbach	23,255,392	NYSE	ZB	35½	23½	30⅞
Diamond Shamrock	14,006,981	NYSE	DIA	23⅛	11⅞	22½
Georgia-Pacific	47,181,607	NYSE	GP	57⅜	37½	57⅛
Great Northern Nekoosa	4,646,482	NYSE	GNN	53½	34¾	43½
Hammermill Paper	5,737,074	NYSE	HML	27¼	17	23½
International Paper	44,313,025	NYSE	IP	40	28⅜	35¼
Kimberly-Clark	23,383,733	NYSE	KMB	39¾	27¼	31
Marcor	25,562,528	NYSE	M	30⅞	18¼	29¼
Masonite	7,777,062	NYSE	MNC	53⅞	24⅞	52⅞
Mead Corp.	16,403,387	NYSE	MEA	21⅞	11	16⅜
Potlatch Forests	7,076,203	NYSE	PFI	39¼	23⅛	28
St. Regis Paper	13,678,000	NYSE	SRT	37⅜	28¼	37¼
Scott Paper	34,455,000	NYSE	SPP	35	21⅛	24
Union Camp	15,039,199	NYSE	UCC	34½	23⅝	30½
U.S. Plywood-Champion	27,902,000	NYSE	UPC	32⅝	21⅜	27¾
Westvaco	10,417,843	NYSE	W	28¾	18¼	23
Weyerhaeuser	60,828,031	NYSE	WY	59	34	57¼

Note: (a) Above outstanding shares are the very latest available figures (in most cases from September 30 to December 31, 1970.

(b) Above prices and shares are adjusted for all stock dividends and/or stock splits effective through December 31, 1970.

PAINE WEBBER INDEX
(For Real Estate Investment Trusts)

The *Paine Webber Index* was prepared by Paine, Webber, Jackson & Curtis in conjunction with the National Association of Real Estate Investment Funds to reflect market price movement of shares of beneficial interest of qualified real estate investment trusts. Recognizing that there are two basic kinds of trusts, the Index is divided into two sections—one for equity trusts and another for mortgage trusts.

In preparing the Paine Webber Index the variable divisor method (see Appendix) was used to compute averages of market prices. This is the same method which is employed in compiling the Dow Jones Averages.

The averages produced have been indexed to a base of 100, using December 30, 1966, as the base date. In order to reflect relative market price movements of equity and mortgage trust shares of beneficial interest since December 30, 1966, the Index has been plotted against the Dow Jones Industrial Average.

Criteria for Selection

On June 30, 1969, thirteen equity trusts and nine mortgage trusts were included in the Index. A trust was included in the Index if its total market value exceeded $10 million in the case of an equity trust or $20 million in the case of a mortgage trust. Total market value is defined as market price times the number of shares of beneficial interest outstanding (exclusive of any shares reserved, but not issued, for possible future issuances, i.e., conversion of convertible securities, exercise of warrants, etc.).

Trusts Included in the Indexes as of July 2, 1970

Equity Trusts

		Date Included in Index
1.	American Realty Trust	12/30/66
2.	Amico Properties	12/30/66
3.	Denver Real Estate Investment Association	12/30/66
4.	First Union Realty Trust	12/30/66
5.	Franklin Realty	12/30/66
6.	Greenfield Real Estate Investment Trust	12/30/66
7.	Kavanau Real Estate Trust	12/30/66
8.	National Realty Investors	12/30/66
9.	Pennsylvania Real Estate Investment Trust	12/30/66
10.	Real Estate Investment Trust of America	12/30/66
11.	U. S. Realty Investments	12/30/66
12.	Washington Real Estate Investment Trust	12/30/66
13.	Hubbard Real Estate Investments	1/08/70
14.	Realty Income Trust	1/08/70
15.	Saul (B.F.) Real Estate Investment Trust	1/08/70

Mortgage Trusts

		Date Included in Index
1.	Continental Mortgage Investors	12/30/66
2.	First Mortgage Investors	12/30/66
3.	General Mortgage Investors	12/31/68
4.	Associated Mortgage Investors	2/14/69
5.	North American Mortgage Investments	2/14/69
6.	Galbreath First Mortgage Investments	3/28/69
7.	Guardian Mortgage Investors	4/15/69
8.	Security Mortgage Investors	4/30/69
9.	Sutro Mortgage Investment Trust	5/29/69
10.	American Century Mortgage Investors	1/8/70
11.	Cameron-Brown Investment Group	1/8/70
12.	City Investing Mortgage Group	1/8/70
13.	Diversified Mortgage Investors	1/8/70
14.	Fidelity Mortgage Investors	1/8/70
15.	Great American Mortgage Investors	1/8/70
16.	Larwin Mortgage Investors	1/8/70
17.	Lomas & Nettleton Mortgage Investors	1/8/70
18.	Medical Mortgage Investors	1/8/70
19.	Mortgage Investment Group	1/8/70
20.	Mortgage Trust of America	1/8/70
21.	Republic Mortgage Investors	1/8/70
22.	MONY Mortgage Investors	7/2/70
23.	Wachovia Realty Investments	7/2/70

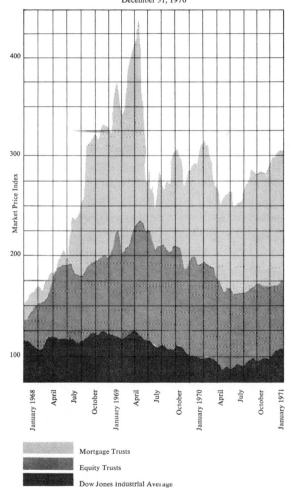

Paine Webber Index
(Base Price on 12/30/66 = 100)
December 31, 1970

PRICE INDEXES

Date	Paine, Webber Equity Trust Index	Paine, Webber Mortgage Trust Index	Dow Jones Industrial Index
December 30, 1966	100	100	100
March 31, 1967	110	122	110
June 30, 1967	110	121	110
September 29, 1967	113	151	118
December 29, 1967	127	149	115
March 15, 1968	152	159	107
June 14, 1968	186	208	116
September 30, 1968	192	309(5)	119
December 31, 1968	196	328(6)	120
March 28, 1969	212	386(6)	119
June 30, 1969	221	271	111
September 25, 1969	203	273	106
December 31, 1969	191	283	102
March 26, 1970	188	312	101
June 25, 1970	160	262	88
September 24, 1970	163	288	97
December 31, 1970	175	306	107

Appendix

Composition of the Index

Trusts whose shares traded publicly prior to January 1, 1969, were included in the Index from December 30, 1966, if they met the stated criteria at any time between January 1, 1969, and May 31, 1969. Trusts whose shares were offered to the public between January 1, 1969, and May 31, 1969, were included in the Index if they met the above criteria on the 30th calendar day after the prospectus date of the public offering. Trusts whose shares are publicly offered (a) as part of a units offering or (b) as a subscription offering are, and in the future will be, included in the Index if they meet the above criteria (a) on the 30th calendar day after the date, as stated in the prospectus, on which the shares are detachable from the other securities in the unit or (b) on the 30th calendar day after the expiration date of the subscription period.

Trusts whose shares traded publicly prior to January 1, 1969, but did not meet the above criteria and trusts whose shares were offered to the public subsequent to May 31, 1969, were reviewed on December 31, 1969, and included in the Index if they met the above criteria on either November 28, 1969, or December 31, 1969, provided that in case of trusts whose shares are offered to the public, thirty calendar days have elapsed from the prospectus date of the public offering. Subsequent to December 31, 1969, trusts will be similarly reviewed semiannually and will be included in the Index if they meet the above criteria 30 days prior to the end of each review period.

A trust will be deleted from the Index if it ceases to qualify as a real estate investment trust or if its investments become significantly different from those of most other equity or mortgage trusts. A trust will not be deleted from the Index, if, due solely to a decline in the market price of its shares, its total market value falls below the criteria stated above.

Bibliography

Beaton, W. *Real Estate Investment.* Prentice-Hall, Inc., 1971.

Berman, Daniel S. *How to Reap Profits in Local Real Estate Syndicates.* Prentice-Hall, Inc., 1964.

Bitney, F. *How to Buy Recreation Land for Profit.* Prentice-Hall, Inc., 1970.

Bohon, Davis T. *Complete Guide to Profitable Real Estate Leasing.* Prentice-Hall, Inc., 1965.

McMichael, S. L., and Moser, Leslie F. *How to Make Money in Real Estate.* Third Edition. Prentice-Hall, Inc.

Nair, G. *Guide to Successful Real Estate Investing.* Prentice-Hall, Inc., 1971.

Reality Enterprise, 2662 Hubbard Road, Madison, Ohio. *Real Estate Investment & Tax Guide.*

Index